How to Rebuild & Modify
CHRYSLER
SLANT SIX
ENGINES

Doug Dutra

CarTech®

CarTech ®

CarTech®, Inc.
838 Lake Street South
Forest Lake, MN 55025
Phone: 651-277-1200 or 800-551-4754
Fax: 651-277-1203
www.cartechbooks.com

Edit by Wes Eisenschenk
Layout by Hailey Samples

ISBN 978-1-61325-432-5
Item No. SA429

Library of Congress Cataloging-in-Publication Data
Names: Dutra, Doug, author.
Title: Chrysler Slant Six engines : how to rebuild and modify / Doug Dutra.
Description: Forest Lake, MN : CarTech, Inc., [2019] | Includes bibliographical references and index.
Identifiers: LCCN 2018041949 | ISBN 9781613254325 (alk. paper)
Subjects: LCSH: Chrysler automobile–Motors–Modification–Handbooks,
  manuals, etc. | Chrysler automobile–Motors–Maintenance and repair–Handbooks, manuals, etc. | LCGFT: Handbooks and manuals.
Classification: LCC TL215.C55 .D88 2019 | DDC 629.25/040288–dc23
LC record available at https://lccn.loc.gov/2018041949

Written, edited, and designed in the U.S.A.
Printed in China
10 9 8 7 6 5 4 3 2 1

DISTRIBUTION BY:

Europe
PGUK
63 Hatton Garden
London EC1N 8LE, England
Phone: 020 7061 1980 • Fax: 020 7242 3725
www.pguk.co.uk

Australia
Renniks Publications Ltd.
3/37-39 Green Street
Banksmeadow, NSW 2109, Australia
Phone: 2 9695 7055 • Fax: 2 9695 7355
www.renniks.com

Canada
Login Canada
300 Saulteaux Crescent
Winnipeg, MB, R3J 3T2 Canada
Phone: 800 665 1148 • Fax: 800 665 0103
www.lb.ca

CONTENTS

WHAT IS A WORKBENCH® BOOK?

This *Workbench®* Series book is the only book of its kind on the market. No other book offers the same combination of detailed hands-on information and revealing color photographs to illustrate engine rebuilding. Rest assured, you have purchased an indispensable companion that will expertly guide you, one step at a time, through each important stage of the rebuilding process. This book is packed with real world techniques and practical tips for expertly performing rebuild procedures, not vague instructions or unnecessary processes. At-home mechanics or enthusiast builders strive for professional results, and the instruction in our *Workbench®* Series books help you realize pro-caliber results. Hundreds of photos guide you through the entire process from start to finish, with informative captions containing comprehensive instructions for every step of the process.

The step-by-step photo procedures also contain many additional photos that show how to install high-performance components, modify stock components for special applications, or even call attention to assembly steps that are critical to proper operation or safety. These are labeled with unique icons. These symbols represent an idea, and photos marked with the icons contain important, specialized information.

Here are some of the icons found in *Workbench®* books:

Important!— Calls special attention to a step or procedure, so that the procedure is correctly performed. This prevents damage to a vehicle, system, or component.

Save Money— Illustrates a method or alternate method of performing a rebuild step that will save money but still give acceptable results.

Torque Fasteners— Illustrates a fastener that must be properly tightened with a torque wrench at this point in the rebuild. The torque specs are usually provided in the step.

Special Tool— Illustrates the use of a special tool that may be required or can make the job easier (caption with photo explains further).

Performance Tip— Indicates a procedure or modification that can improve performance. Step most often applies to high-performance or racing engines.

Critical Inspection— Indicates that a component must be inspected to ensure proper operation of the engine.

Precision Measurement— Illustrates a precision measurement or adjustment that is required at this point in the rebuild.

Professional Mechanic Tip— Illustrates a step in the rebuild that non-professionals may not know. It may illustrate a shortcut, or a trick to improve reliability, prevent component damage, etc.

Documentation Required— Illustrates a point in the rebuild where the reader should write down a particular measurement, size, part number, etc. for later reference or photograph a part, area or system of the vehicle for future reference.

Tech Tip— Tech Tips provide brief coverage of important subject matter that doesn't naturally fall into the text or step-by-step procedures of a chapter. Tech Tips contain valuable hints, important info, or outstanding products that professionals have discovered after years of work. These will add to your understanding of the process, and help you get the most power, economy, and reliability from your engine.

A *big* thank-you to my family and Slant Six friends who encouraged me in my "hobby" and passion for everything Slant Six.

Special thanks to my wife and children for supporting me while we relocated to Sonoma County, California and built a new house, and for helping Dad as he wrote this book.

Countless "Slant Sixers" and other automotive enthusiasts also helped with this effort, but individual acknowledgment must be given to Steve Magnante, Dan Stern, and the staff at TorqStorm for their direct contributions to this publication.

ABOUT THE AUTHOR

Doug Dutra (aka Doctor Dodge) is the middle child of five kids (four boys and a girl). His grandfather and father always drove various Chrysler, Dodge, and Plymouth vehicles, so it was a given that the Dutra children would also drive Mopars when they reached driving age. Kids in the Dutra family had to purchase, register, insure, and maintain their own vehicles. This was no easy task for a young driver in the early 1970s. The Chrysler A-Body cars (the Dodge Dart, Lancer, and Demon, the Plymouth Valiant, Duster, and Barracuda) sold well in the 1960s and 1970s, many of them with Slant Six engines, so they were plentiful and great used cars for young drivers with little money or automotive knowledge.

Doug's first car in high school was a 1963 Dodge Dart station wagon powered by a 170 Slant Six with a 3-on-the-tree manual transmission. The engine and transmission were soon swapped to a 340 Six-Pak and 4-speed setup that his older brother located. By the end of the 1970s, Doug's hot rod Dart wagon had a Slant Six back in it, so it is safe to say that there was a good amount of automotive wrenching going on at the Dutra house. During this time, Doug became proficient in general automotive repair work but really excelled in Chrysler engine rebuilding. His engine-rebuilding expertise started with the Mopar muscle car high-performance V-8 engines of the era, but many of the family's daily driver cars were Slant Six powered, so he rebuilt a few of those engines as well.

In the 1980s, Doug was still driving his Slant Six, 4-speed 1963 Dart wagon, which always seemed to get him where he needed to go. During that time, he gained more

Doug Dutra (aka Doctor Dodge or "Doc") has owned and worked on Chrysler products all his life. Doug is best known for his intimate knowledge of the Slant Six and for creating cast-iron split exhaust manifolds for the engine (Dutra Duals). He is also responsible for reproducing a small number of the legendary Hyper-Pak intake manifold, used in early compact car NASCAR races. Doug is shown next to his fully restored 1965 Dodge Dart GT, powered by an aluminum-block Slant Six.

appreciation of the Slant Six and started applying his hot rod V-8 engine-rebuilding experience to it. The performance increases he found in the Slant Six were impressive, and they led him to the drag strip, where he tested his combinations. Doug started developing 6-cylinder performance parts and shared his Slant Six engine hop-up success with the Slant Six club and various Mopar magazines of the time.

By 1990, Doug was making custom cast-iron dual exhaust manifolds (Dutra Duals). Later, he began building a reproduction long ram Hyper-Pak intake manifold for the Slant Six. All the racetrack testing showed him that a Slant Six could be converted into a real performance engine and that there was still some genuine interest. He soon found others who enjoyed racing a unique engine and liked its underdog following. Organizing Slant Six races and car shows was the next step, and by doing so, Doug met and collaborated with many other Slant Six enthusiasts.

Someone once said "If you do something long enough, you will become the expert," and that's what happened as Doug took all his Slant Six knowledge into the 21st century. He worked with like-minded people to get the slant six.org website started, and through more engine building and racing, *Slant Six Racing News* was born. That publication helped develop a SlantSix–only bracket racing class and points series at national Mopar drag race events. These efforts have moved the engine from its stodgy daily-driver reputation toward a performance and "dare to be different" standing. We are confident that Doug will continue to develop, test, and support the Chrysler Slant Six as we move through the years ahead.

FOREWORD BY STEVE MAGNANTE

Even though it has been nearly 40 years, I can still hear it if I concentrate: the childhood sound-memory of my neighbor Jake's Dodge A100 window van starting on cold winter mornings in rural Massachusetts. Though Jake's driveway was more than a quarter mile from my bedroom window, the frigid air readily carried the unique chirping sound of its Chrysler starter motor, then the guttural buzz as the van's 225 Slant Six coughed to life. Though built in 1967 and barely 10 years old at the time, the van's two-tone blue and white body was badly rusted from constant exposure to New England road salt. The muffler was even rustier, riddled with holes and burst at the seam. Exhaust noise was amplified—not dulled.

From my pillow, I could immediately tell if it was Jake or his girlfriend, Martha, at the wheel. If it was Jake, the engine settled into a steady high idle after only a few tries. Then I could hear the deft applications of throttle as he backed it out onto the street, put the TorqueFlite into Drive, and slowly rumbled past my window on his way to work. Jake was an old hand at driving Slant Sixes in the winter. He understood the art of tickling the carburetor with a light foot to prevent stalling.

On the other hand, if Martha was at the wheel, as soon as the engine lit off she'd hold the gas pedal down, way down. She figured it was all the quicker to get hot air from the heater on a single-digit winter morning. What she didn't understand was the molasses-thick motor oil and the dead-cold engine probably weren't happy running at 3,500 rpm mere moments after initial start-up. But she got away with it again and again. In fact, that old A100 van served Jake and Martha for many years before rust separated the steering box from the frame. Sure enough, it was replaced by another one, a windowless brown A108 stretch-wheelbase model also powered by a 225 Slant Six.

When my friends and I got to be of driving age around 1980, we had at our disposal a vast array of Slant Six–powered hand-me-down cars to choose from. I lost track of the many push-button Darts, four-door Signets, crusty Dusters, and big-glass Barracudas we went through. Though most were rusty and suffering from that chronic Mopar malady, the rotted torsion bar crossmember, a few were very well preserved and should have been saved. I remember my pal Bruce's light green 1968 Barracuda fastback. Completely rust free, it would be a valuable car today if he hadn't plowed it into a tree in 1984.

Then there was Jimmy's 1970 Challenger, born a C-code 225 machine. He bought it off the back lot of a local Dodge dealer for $400, a bunch of money at a time when an average beater cost only $20 to $150. Again, it was only a decade old, but the thick layer of black undercoating applied to the entire underhood area by the seller should have alerted us to its rusty nature. But it was a factory FJ5 Sublime Green car (with a watery respray), and he was dazzled and drove it away. I still remember the shotgun blast effect when the driver-side torsion bar anchor released its stored energy one night. The front suspension immediately settled onto the jounce rubbers. The passenger-side torsion bar mount let go soon after, and Jimmy never repaired the rusted torsion bar sockets. Instead, he drove it for another year, its nonexistent front suspension bashing and crashing over the bumpy roads in our small town. Amazingly, not a single police officer

Steve Magnante is a well-known automotive journalist and television personality with an interest in and appreciation for the unusual. Steve has always enjoyed Chrysler products and has a fondness for the Slant Six, especially the aluminum-block version. Steve and Doug have collaborated over the years on a number of Slant Six engine build articles that have appeared in Hot Rod, Car Craft, Mopar Muscle, and other online publications.

stopped Jimmy to explore why the Challenger's nose sat so low to the ground.

Looking back, we were ignorant, and those poor old Mopars truly suffered at our young hands. I guess the only saving grace is how rusty most of them were. The junkyard was one stop away for most of them. And sadly, I remember over and over how their Slant Six hearts still ran when they finally entered the scrap yard. Rust (and goonish kids like us)—not poor engineering—was their downfall.

Today, I am older and (I like to think) wiser. I now recognize that Chrysler engineers, including Willem Weertman, Robert Rarey, Tom Hoover, Paul Ackerman, and many others, worked a miracle of sorts with the Slant Six. Their best efforts to devise a tough, flexible, and economical powerplant were at the core of its

ability to absorb our youthful abuse (and my neighbor Martha's brutal 3,500-rpm wintertime warm-ups).

In this book, I am pleased to know that lifelong Slant Six innovator, journalist, enthusiast, and builder Doug Dutra has shared his deep knowledge of the "leaning tower of power." His work ensures that present and future generations can truly understand just how special this engine family is and that it is worthy of continued praise, study, and development.

I first saw Doug's name and writing in back issues of Slant 6 News, the official quarterly magazine of the Slant 6 Club of America that was founded in 1980. I'm somewhat ashamed to admit that Doug and fellow Slant 6 Club members Jack Poehler, Ed Yost, Bob Stepp, and others were hip to the need to preserve these unique engines and cars at the

Steve is shown "exercising" his Slant Six Hyper-Pak-powered 1962 Valiant. This car was used to showcase and test a number of Slant Six engines over the years, and the car ran mid-13-second quarter-mile passes with some combinations. This car found its way onto eBay and ended up going to Australia. Steve's current Slant Six is a 1963 Dodge Dart that he continues to develop and restore.

very time I and my friends were driving them into the dirt.

As penance, and because it's a darned good engine, I have since done all I can to cheerlead the Slant Six in car magazines such as *Hot Rod, Car Craft, Mopar Muscle,* and *Hemmings Classic Car.* At the start of my Slant Six writing around the year 1998, I sought Doug's advice and assistance, and he has never failed to come through with whatever I've needed. In particular, during a Slant Six story being completed for *Mopar Muscle* magazine, Doug took a long weekend away from his busy work and family life to drive more than 300 miles from his home in Sunnyvale, California, to Los Angeles to help me out.

Beyond that, Doug puts his money where his mouth is. Recognizing the fact somebody needed to reproduce the legendary Hyper-Pak ram-tuned intake manifold, Doug made it happen—on his own dime. He also devised a two-piece cast-iron exhaust manifold (Dutra Duals) that forever solved the problems with cracked factory exhaust manifolds and tube steel headers. Word has it Doug may be conjuring an aluminum cylinder head for the Slant Six. All I know is that if anyone can make it happen, Dutra's the man.

Dear reader, enjoy every page of this book as much as Doug enjoyed writing it.

INTRODUCTION

The goal with this book is to document Slant Six engine information gained over the more than 40 years I have worked on this engine. There is some development history included so the reader understands how an engine can end up overengineered, to the point of becoming one of the most robust engines ever built, but I do not intend to go into the engine's ongoing advancement history and eventual demise. I will cover all the basic Slant Six engine configurations released into production and present information on how to correctly identify those engines using casting numbers, ID stampings, and visual clues. I will also show major engine components and the differences that distinguish them, but I cannot show all the application differences that were used to install the Slant Six into a wide range of vehicles and equipment.

Rebuilding an engine is a big, expensive job, so I will give some attention to engine evaluation with the hope that you can get your engine running well by doing a simple tune-up or valve adjustment. The "keep it simple" thinking also applies to the tools used in this book. I will try to show you ways to do a task with the tools you have, instead of the special factory tools shown in the Factory Service Manuals. I will show you some special tools needed to perform specific tasks on a Slant Six, but the focus will be on items that are inexpensive and readily available or that can be rented or made at home with common materials. I will not spend a lot of time or photos on machine shop equipment and processes because most Slant Six owners are going to select a machine shop, take their engine to that shop, and have a professional machinist do the precision engine machine work for them. Look elsewhere if you want to see photos of a crankshaft grinder, engine bore and honing equipment, or other specialized machine shop tools.

The steps for engine removal, breakdown, and inspection will be covered in sequence as I perform the disassembly. The particular sequences shown were chosen so your work is easier and time is not wasted. I want to support a do-it-yourselfer who has access to basic tools and is working on a street-driven vehicle, so the engine rebuild I show here will be a "pump gas" engine, not a race engine. There will be some measurements that you need to take during disassembly and reassembly, but I want to keep those to a minimum and do these measurements in a simple way with common inspection tools.

Engine assembly, installation, and initial start-up will also have an important sequence of operations that should be followed. I will share additional tips and tricks to address the special needs found when working on a Slant Six for the first time. As a bonus, I will review some currently available performance parts and special Slant Six engine combinations that I have tried, in case the owner wants to go to the next step and squeeze more power out of his or her engine. In summary, I want to share all the Slant Six–specific engine rebuilding details I have learned over the years and deliver understandable information to the owner of a street-driven Slant Six vehicle who has some mechanical ability and a set of basic tools.

CHRYSLER SLANT SIX HISTORY

The Chrysler Slant Six engine concept was a direct result of Chrysler's desire to enter an emerging compact car market. The Valiant program started in 1957, and Chrysler did not have an engine that was suitable for that type of vehicle. Low vehicle cost and high fuel economy were required; the 277-ci small-block Chrysler V-8 of the time was too large for the compact car's platform, and its 230-ci L-head (flathead) 6-cylinder engine was outdated with low power and poor fuel efficiency.

V-200 FOUR DOOR SEDAN

V-200 SUBURBAN

V-100 FOUR DOOR SEDAN

V-100 SUBURBAN

Initial Engine Design Work

The new 1960 Valiant had to be a smaller vehicle that could hold up to six passengers, have a reduced frontal area, and be lightweight for improved fuel economy and performance. These requirements would need a short engine with a low profile. Initial Valiant engine concepts included a 150-ci overhead-valve, a cast-iron inline-6, an aluminum V-6 design, and an aluminum inline-6.

170 and 225 ci

An inline-6 engine design with a maximum of 170 ci was preferred by

The new 1960 Valiant started life as its own brand under the Chrysler Corporation umbrella. This vehicle led to an all-new-design inline 6-cylinder engine that we now know as the Chrysler Slant Six.

the Chrysler Engine Design department and looked favorable in early design studies. By May 1958, there was a request to have a larger version of the proposed Valiant inline-6 engine design so it could be used to replace the aging 230-ci L-head 6-cylinder in all Chrysler vehicles. The Engine Design team raised the 170's block deck and added 1 inch of stroke to the concept while using the same bore, cylinder head, and other supporting components. This resulted in a 225-ci engine.

The newly developed 170 and 225 inline-6 bore size, spacing, and crankshaft design were all interrelated, and this had the biggest impact on the engine's overall size and length. A relatively small bore diameter of 3.4 inches and a crankshaft with four main bearings were the result. A large 2.75-inch main bearing size was selected because it was already in use on the 383- and 413-ci Chrysler big-block engines and because the large size was needed to avoid bending and torsional stress problems that were sometimes encountered with a four-main crankshaft in a long-stroke engine. The 2.75-inch main bearing size was overkill for the 170, but it was used anyway in order to standardize the tooling and parts used on both engines.

The desire to standardize parts used in the new inline-6 family is also seen in the cam and cam timing components. The crankshaft's timing chain gear, the timing chain, and the lifter diameter are the same as the ones used in the Chrysler big-block engines released shortly before the Slant Six. The initial designs used bottom-loading mushroom-style lifters and a higher camshaft location carried over from the L-head 6-cylinder. The possible need to use hydraulic

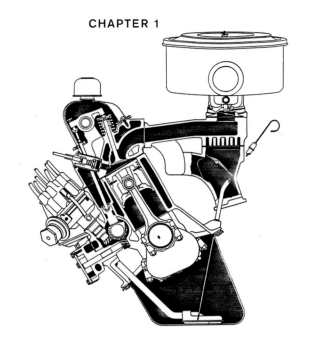

The Slant Six design shows the low position of the oil pump and distributor with both items being driven directly off a gear hobbed into the center of the camshaft. The signature 30-degree slant shows how this idea allowed for a longer runner intake and exhaust manifold while keeping the engine compact and narrow. (Photo Courtesy Bill Weertman)

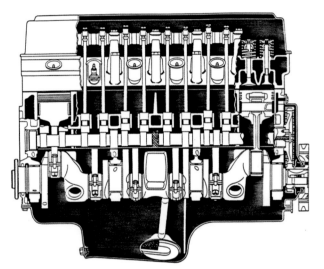

Large-diameter Chrysler big-block lifters were designed into the new Slant Six. The large crankshaft and its four main bearings are big-block sized. Special attention was given to the position of the water pump and the low-profile harmonic damper. This was done to keep the engine's length as short as possible. (Photo Courtesy Bill Weertman)

The single-wall thickness between the cylinder bores and the camshaft tunnel was done to keep the engine narrow and to position the camshaft so a Mopar big-block timing chain could be used. This thin wall later became an obstacle to any significant bore size or engine displacement increases to the Slant Six.

lifters in an aluminum-block engine and to have the lifters load from the top led to the 170's and 225's final design. The lifter style and the camshaft's final location took considerable engineering efforts. Eventually, the Slant Six's final camshaft location would become a limitation for future displacement increases because the cam's location is close to the underside of the cylinder bores.

The locations for the fuel pump, distributor, oil pump, and main oil feed gallery were also based on the plan to produce the engine block using an aluminum die-casting process. The decision to locate the oil pump and distributor in the center of the engine block on the camshaft side was due to the desire to drive the oil pump and distributor directly from a single gear hobbed onto the camshaft. This location also kept the branches of the main oil galleries an even length, providing retraction of long oil gallery–forming core pins from an aluminum engine die-casting mold.

The 30-degree slant to the newly designed engine came about as engineers worked to keep the engine as short and low as possible when installed in the new Valiant's chassis. The idea started with moving the water pump off to one side from the front of the engine. This led to slanting the engine so the water pump's shaft would stay close to the vehicle's chassis centerline. The choice was made to tilt the engine to the right to give room for the steering box and steering column shaft. The tilt to the right also allowed room for longer branches on the intake and exhaust manifolds.

A 30-degree angle was selected because it was a reasonable compromise of width, height, and access to

the distributor, oil pump, and fuel pump, which were all mounted on the right (underslant) side of the engine. Other angles were reviewed, but, in the end, exactly 30 degrees was selected in order to simplify the design calculations and drafting efforts.

Chrysler Engineering designated the letter "G" for the new Slant Six engine family with G or LG (Low G) being used for the 170 ci and RG (Raised G) used for the 225 ci. A patent was then issued on the engine configuration under the name of the lead engineer Fred Rose.

The Die-Cast Aluminum-Block 225 Program

During the initial design period of the Slant Six engine, the automotive industry had a focus on lighter weight vehicles. This focus pushed the Chrysler Engine Design team to make many design decisions based on the new inline-6 being made of aluminum.

Besides weight savings, there would be machining advantages with aluminum, including reducing machining stock material thicknesses, using higher machine speeds and feeds, and having less tool wear and breakage. Of the methods used for making aluminum parts, high-pressure die casting was considered best for accuracy and for high-volume production. The goal was to design the die-cast engine components so many features could be used as cast without further machining. Where machining was required, material thicknesses were kept to a minimum. The Engine Design team had the view that the new Valiant could have a lightweight aluminum engine with little to no

cost penalty compared to a cast-iron engine block.

It was recognized that developing and manufacturing a die-cast aluminum cylinder block and cylinder head involved major risk. At the time, there were no high-volume suppliers for this type of part. As a result, cast-iron versions of the new block and head design were done in parallel. This applied to the 170 and the 225 concept, so Chrysler now had four related inline-6 engines in simultaneous development: 170 and 225, iron and aluminum, with the primary design focus on the two aluminum-block versions. The focus on using the weaker aluminum material resulted in design features that were well beyond requirements when carried over into a cast-iron engine block design.

Cylinder Blocks

The die-cast aluminum cylinder blocks were designed with an open top deck. They used cast-in-place cast-iron cylinder liners that stood 7 inches tall in the water jacket area. The block was extended below the crankshaft's centerline to add beam structure. The crankshaft was held in place by upper and lower cast-iron main bearing caps to control main bearing oil clearances throughout the engine's operating temperature range.

The rear main seal also received an upper main seal retainer cap. This was done to simplify the block's crankshaft pocket machining work. The cylinder head and the main bearing cap bolts used on the aluminum blocks have a longer threaded area to reduce the chance of stripping the threads out of the mating tapped holes in aluminum.

These are the significant

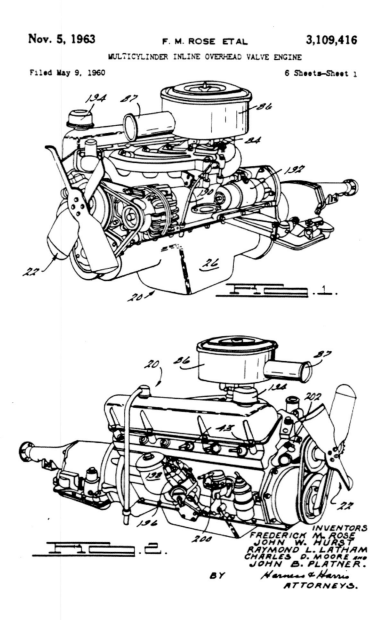

Nov. 5, 1963   F. M. ROSE ET AL   3,109,416

MULTICYLINDER INLINE OVERHEAD VALVE ENGINE

Filed May 9, 1960   6 Sheets—Sheet 1

INVENTORS
FREDERICK M. ROSE
JOHN W. HURST
RAYMOND L. LATHAM
CHARLES D. MOORE and
JOHN B. PLATNER.
BY
ATTORNEYS.

Left: US patent number 3109416 listed the inventors and the filing attorneys. Willem L. Weertman was the chief engineer responsible for this new engine. (Photo Courtesy Bill Weertman)

The new Slant Six was initially designed to be made from aluminum in order to reduce the engine's weight. Designers also believed that a die-cast aluminum engine block would increase production speed and decrease block machining time and tool wear.

The manifold side of the die-cast aluminum Slant Six engine block shows the lack of freeze plugs and the contours around six individual cylinders. The water pump's mounting flange location was moved to the side of the block so the engine's length could be minimized.

differences in the aluminum versus cast-iron cylinder block designs. All other major engine parts were the same in the aluminum and cast-iron block Slant Six engines.

The weight savings focus would also find its way into other bolt-on engine component designs. The cylinder head, intake manifold, water pump housing, oil pump housing, and thermostat cover were all designed as die-cast or sandcast aluminum parts.

Changes over the Production Years

The basic Slant Six design and structure (overall dimensions, bolt patterns, etc.) went unchanged during its 31-year production history. This means a cylinder head, manifold, oil pan, and other parts from a 1960 170 Slant Six will bolt onto a 225 engine produced in 1987. With that said, there were continual internal and external changes being made to improve and refine the engine during its

production run.

A list of major events and basic changes made to the engine follows. This is by no means a complete list covering all the Slant Six engine variations developed for different applications, chassis, and markets, but it can be used as a general guide for the enthusiast looking for the best Slant Six engine for their intended use.

170- and 225-ci Internal and External Changes

Year	Changes
1960	Start of production for cast-iron 170-ci and 225-ci engines.
1961	Production release of 225-ci aluminum-block engines.
	Intake manifolds changed from aluminum to cast iron.
	Alternator moved from left side to right side of engine.
	Last year of the Hyper-Pak engine option.
	A 225-ci engine was added to the Valiant as an option.
1963	Last year of the aluminum 225-ci engine.
	PCV valve used on all Slant Six engines.
1964	Created a 100-percent closed crankcase vent system in California.
1967	A 2-barrel intake manifold and carburetor setup is offered for export engines.
	Cylinder head combustion chamber shape is modified for improved combustion.
1968	Crankshaft rear flange counterbore size increased.
	Closed crankcase venting on all engines.
1969	Last year of 170-ci engine availability for US and Canada market.
1970	Start of 198-ci engine production.
1972	Exhaust valve seats are induction hardened.
	Air injection added to California engines.
1973	EGR valve added.
1974	The last year of 198-ci engine production.
1975	New cylinder head: taper-seat spark plugs with no plug tubes.
1976	General weight reduction.
	Aluminum intake manifold for Feather Duster/Dart Light.
	Forged-steel crankshaft changed to nodular cast iron in mid-1976 production.
1977	A 2-barrel intake and carb option added to domestic engines.
1978	Intake manifold changed from cast iron to aluminum.
1981	Hydraulic lifters introduced that had nonadjustable rocker arms and a wide valve cover.
1983	Last year of domestic passenger car Slant Six engine use.
1984	Last year of Slant Six engine production at the Trenton Engine Plant.
	Additional weight reduction on the cast-iron crankshaft.
1987	Last year of Slant Six engine use in domestic trucks.
1991	Last year of Slant Six engine production at the Toluca, Mexico, engine plant.

The engine block's casting number is located on the driver's side of the block. The engine's build numbers are stamped into a pad on the front passenger's side of the block's head gasket surface. These numbers are the best way to identify the engine and the production date, but the casting and stamped-in numbers can sometimes be missing or misleading. Besides the numbers, there are other easy-to-spot engine block features that can help you quickly identify a Slant Six.

170-ci Cast Iron (1960–1969)

Low-deck 170-ci cast-iron block Slant Six engines (LG designation) with forged-steel crankshafts (FC) were built between 1960 and 1969. All of the 170 engines used forged cranks with a 3.125-inch stroke. The distance between the top head gasket surface and the crankshaft centerline (deck height) is 9.06 inches. The 170 block casting number was 2463230, and that number was located on the driver's side of the block.

All 170-ci blocks had three freeze plugs, with the center plug being 2.25 inches higher than the outer two.

Engine Identification

There are five basic Slant Six engine cylinder block types that were released into production. Four are made of cast iron and one is an aluminum die casting. The different cast-iron blocks produced can make it confusing when you're trying to figure out exactly which engine you have in your vehicle or which engine you spotted at a swap meet or in a wrecking yard.

Slant Six engine blocks can all look the same at a distance, but there were actually five different block types used over the years.

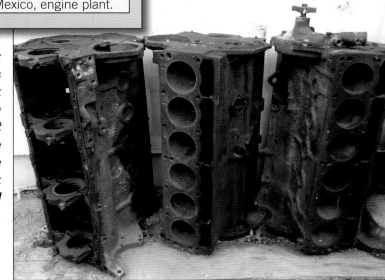

Revell Quarter-Scale Slant Six Model Kit Story

by Steve Magnante
with Willem "Bill" Weertman

Since most car enthusiasts caught the automotive bug early in life, thanks to plastic model kits, it seemed appropriate to review one of the most interesting and complex plastic model kits in history: Revell's quarter-scale Slant Six engine and transmission.

Introduced in the fall of 1961 and produced for about two years, Revell kit number H-1553:1295 cost a hefty $12.95 when it was new. At that time, a typical 1/25-scale car model kit was priced at well under two bucks. Thanks to its incredible realism, the Revell engine kit required an advanced level of skill. Mixing those two things together (high cost and the need to get Dad involved), the Revell kit wasn't a huge success. The one thing that saved it from likely oblivion was Chrysler Corporation's direct involvement in the project. That meant the full weight of Chrysler's public relations and marketing departments was called upon to spread the word. As a result, Chrysler sponsored full-page ads promoting the kit in magazines ranging from *Hot Rod* to *Life* and even nudged magazine editors to publish new product alerts and actual editorial stories, including the one that appeared in the September 1961 issue of *Rod & Custom* magazine.

Even if it wasn't a hobby shop sales record setter, the Revell Slant Six model kit got first-class exposure that continues here in Doug Dutra's much-needed Slant Six book. Let's explore a vintage Revell Slant Six kit that was purchased on eBay. If you search "revell slant six" online, you'll see the impact left by this great Revell model kit.

We reached out to Willem Weertman for his memories about the Revell Slant Six model kit program, and he shared some amazing memories.

Bill Weertman worked directly with Revell to ensure that the 1/4-scale model of the Slant Six was as accurate as possible. (All Photos Courtesy Steve Magnante)

If Weertman's name isn't immediately familiar, know that he was Chrysler's assistant chief engineer during the Slant Six and Chrysler Street Hemi development programs.

If you've ever read the iconic "Hemi White Paper" article in the August 1966 issue of *Hot Rod* magazine, you'll recognize Weertman's face and his informative yet personable writing style. As a Chrysler employee, he worked directly with the Revell modelers as the liaison between them and Chrysler engineering. The following is Bill's commentary on his part in developing the Revell Slant Six model kit:

"The Revell Slant Six model kit had an interesting start. Sometime after production of the Slant Six engine began and the engine was a fresh newcomer on the automotive scene, an executive of Chrysler corporate advertising and a public relations executive of Revell, Inc., a company well known for its accurate scale models, especially of ships, happened to meet at an adver-

tising industry function (reportedly a hospitality party). In talking about their respective products, the idea was hatched between the two executives for Revell, with technical support from Chrysler, to make a scale model of the Slant Six engine.

"It would not simply be a static model of the exterior of the engine but a model with all the parts, which could actually be motored to show internal parts in motion. That would give the builders of the model quite an education in the workings of an automotive engine as well an introduction to a distinctive Chrysler product.

"The Chrysler advertising executive secured the cooperation of the top Chrysler engineering executives. In early 1960, as managing engineer of the Engine Design Department, I was asked to send Revell whatever it needed for the project. On April 20, 1960, we sent a complete set of drawings of the 170-ci Slant Six engine so they could start work on a 1/4-size scale model of the engine. In addition to the drawings, I think they were also furnished an actual engine assembly.

"Over the next several months, I would occasionally receive inquiries by phone from my Revell contact, their chief engineer. By February 1961, Revell had a prototype of the engine model kit ready to show to distributors and dealers that would be attending the annual weeklong Hobby Industry Trade Show in Chicago. For the Revell booth at the show, Chrysler shipped one of its own cutaway, motor-driven Slant Six display engines. I was asked to give a short, private talk about the engine to the Revell people who were there for the show and to attend the booth along with the Revell staff to answer questions about the engine. I helped man the booth and found the Revell group to be very friendly and interesting; we got along just fine.

"Revell sent me one of the very first pilot production kits with a request that I assemble the engine and send back any comments I might have. Well, I made the assembly with some judicious filing and sanding to get the plastic parts to fit together properly and then found the engine looked okay but had so much friction that the small battery-driven electric motor didn't have a chance to put the internal parts in motion. So I made a complete disassembly followed by additional filing and sanding for running clearance improvement and then a reassembly. This time success. The engine came alive with the crankshaft rotating, the pistons going up and down, valves opening and closing, and the miniature lightbulbs representing spark plugs turning on and off in the correct sequence. Wow!

"Revell had very skillfully designed the model so that when the removable pieces that included the intake and exhaust manifolds and the left side of

the cylinder head and the left side of the cylinder block were lifted away, the internal action was exposed for viewing. I sent Revell a detailed report on my experience assembling the engine. I don't know if any revisions were made to the engine parts before high-volume production began. Years later, I gave my assembled model to the Chrysler archives.

"Full production of the model engine started in the fall of 1961, in time for the Christmas-buying season. In addition to assembly instructions, each boxed kit had an eight-page booklet describing the basic workings of an internal combustion engine, reinforcing the educational aspect of the model.

"After sales started, quite a few letters arrived on my desk from model builders all over the country with complimentary comments and interest in additional information about Chrysler engines. I continued communicating with Revell, sending them engineering drawings of possible future changes to the Slant Six engine, including the aluminum cylinder block version and the change in crankcase ventilation from the original road draft tube to the positive crankcase ventilation system that was used 100 percent in 1963 after being a California-only requirement in 1961 and 1962. There was some consideration for their updating the model to reflect production changes made to the real engine. However, as far as I know nothing ever came of this, and to the best of my knowledge the model was unchanged during its production run. For me it was a fun project with lasting good memories and a nice bit of personal recognition."

—Bill Weertman, July 6, 2007

The assembled model measures 14¾ inches from fan blade to tail shaft and about 7 inches from oil pan to air cleaner. While most assume

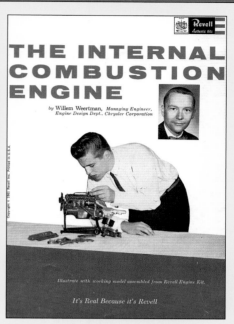

An eight-page educational booklet on how an internal combustion engine works was included in the Revell Slant Six model kits.

The assembled model is shown on the stand provided. The kits we found came with the original box.

the kit is based on a 225-ci Slant Six, Weertman tells us it is actually based on the low-deck 170-ci Slant Six. The massive box measures 22x14¾ and is 3 inches deep.

Revell Quarter-Scale Slant Six Model Kit Story *(continued)*

There are no fewer than four shades of plastic: red, silver, gray, and black. They are used in the kit to reduce the need for painting. Full-color decals adorn the air and oil filters as well as the display stand.

Cleverly hidden inside the beautifully rendered A903 3-speed manual transmission lurks a small battery-operated electric motor that turns the crank, rods, pistons, rocker arms, and valves when the power button is pushed.

Four small screws secure the transmission to the bellhousing. The beauty of the Revell Slant Six model is that it can be disassembled and rebuilt time and time again. The intake and exhaust tract simply snaps into the side of the cylinder head, and nuts and screws hold the rest of the kit's approximately 300 parts together. The entire driver-side wall of the block is removable to expose the cylinder bores and pistons.

The following photos show the intricate details contained in this model kit. One example is the completely flat valve cover, a characteristic of the 1960-only 170-ci Slant Six, which the kit was designed from. ∎

A slotted drive coupler inside the bellhousing plugs into the motorized "transmission."

The piston rings were made in different colors of plastic: red for compression rings and green for the oil control rings.

All of the parts in this exploded view can be snapped back in place within a matter of seconds. Tiny metal screws secure the valve cover and oil pan. Dig the correct unsilenced air cleaner; only the front half of the filter was shielded from water mist. Fully enclosed air cleaner lids arrived in 1962.

Many pieces can be removed to show cutaway details on internal parts.

The detailed cylinder head even bears a casting number (2121476-4), correct for a 1960 cast-iron Slant Six. Note the detailed rocker arm shafts, valve springs, and rocker arms. This is just like the real thing.

The combustion chamber and valve head detail is totally accurate. The intake and exhaust port floors are cast integrally with the intake and exhaust manifold segment. Check out the tiny screws attaching the bellhousing to the block.

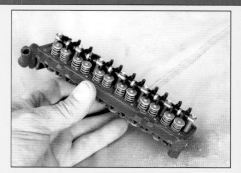

This shot gives an idea of how large this model is. The valves move smoothly in the guides, and the metal valve springs still have good tension, even after being on display for decades.

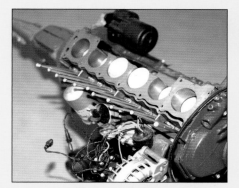

Yep, there are even individual lifters and pushrods inside the engine.

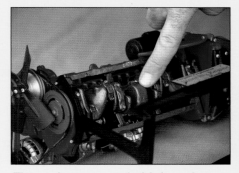

The main caps are held down by metal bolts while real nut and screw fasteners secure the rod caps. The crankshaft is also shaped and contoured just like a forged-steel production piece and even has the rough finish on the counterweights.

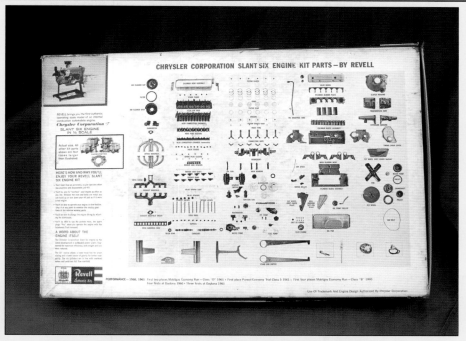

The bottom of the box features a complete parts inventory list with photos of every item. The two kits purchased got us far, but we still have not seen an original instruction sheet nor have we seen the original Revell battery box that came with the kit.

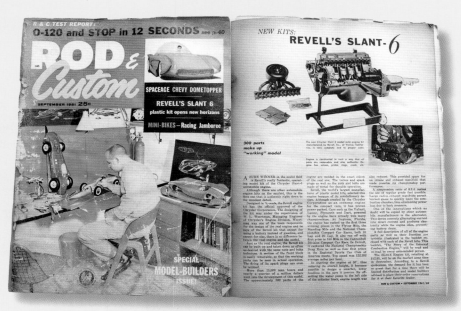

The September 1961 issue of Rod & Custom contained a full-page look-see story on the kit. The article states that more than 15,000 man-hours and a quarter of a million dollars went into the development of this 300-piece model kit. We believe it!

The cylinder block's casting number is located on the manifold side of the engine block below the freeze plugs. The dash number shown after the seven-digit casting number relates to the casting patterns used to make that block.

The engine build stamping is often missing on replacement engine blocks or blocks that have been rebuilt. These stamped numbers get machined away if you resurface the block's deck surface. Copy down your engine's markings before you deck the block, then restamp as needed.

Block deck resurfacing can erase the stamped build numbers, and casting flaws can make the casting numbers hard to read or confusing. This five–freeze plug 225 engine block should carry casting number 2806830, but it is missing the second 8.

All 170-ci Slant Six engine blocks carry casting number 2463230-XX. The 170 has a zero-deck height, which means the pistons come to the top of the cylinder bores. This 170 block casting number is followed by a "-1", which is the reference to the casting equipment used to make the block. Other markings include a date code and the production shift that produced the casting. This block also carries a rebuilder's ID tag that was added when the engine was rebuilt.

All 170 Slant Six engine blocks have three freeze plugs, with the center plug positioned higher than the outer two freeze plugs. All 170 engines used forged-steel crankshafts, so the gusset behind the water pump is tapered.

The 170-ci engine block had a shorter height, so the assembled engine sat lower in the vehicle's engine compartment. To the trained eye, the bare block appeared shorter, but the easy-to-spot feature was the shorter (1.75-inch) coolant bypass hose between the cylinder head and the water pump. The other tip was the 1×3/4×5/8-inch-thick cast-in rectangle at the top of the driver's side of the cylinder deck. On the low-deck

Five Production Slant Six Cylinder Block Types

CI	Material	Freeze Plugs	Color	Deck Rectangle	Flange	Gusset B. Hose	Notes
170	Iron	3	Red	On Water Pump	Angled	1.75 inches	
225	Iron	3	Red	1.5-inch space	Angled	3.75 inches	
225	Iron	5	Blue	1.5-inch space	Angled	3.75 inches	Used on 198 ci
225	Iron	5	Blue	1.5-inch space	Straight	3.75 inches	"E" in ID Stamping
225	Aluminum	None	Red	1.5-inch space	Straight (2)	3.75 inches	

The 170-ci engine block was shorter, so the short coolant bypass hose is an easy way to identify a 170 Slant Six. All 170 engines have forged-steel crankshafts and carry casting number 2463230.

A 170 Slant Six engine block is shorter than a 225 or 198 block. Look at the area where the water pump meets the top deck and head gasket surface as a way to spot the difference.

170, this rectangle sits directly on the water pump's mounting flange.

225-ci Cast Iron (1960–1967)

The high-deck 225 cast-iron block Slant Six (RG designation) with a forged-steel crank (RGFC) had a 10.70-inch deck height and a 4.125-inch stroke. The forged-crankshaft Slant Six engine blocks were

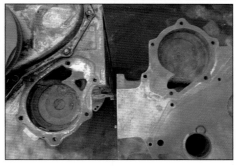

A side-by-side comparison between a 170 and a 225 engine block shows how much shorter a 170 Slant Six engine block is.

produced in two distinct castings. An early three–freeze plug version (with the center plug being 2.25 inches higher than the outer two) was produced between 1960 and 1967. The early 225 block casting number was 2463430, and it was located on the driver's side of the block.

198- and 225-ci RGFC (1968–1976)

The later RGFC block with casting number 2806830 was produced between 1968 and 1976. This block type was used to build both 198- and 225-ci Slant Six engines. RGFC blocks had five freeze plugs all in a row with all at the same height.

The easily spotted feature for the RG-type engine blocks was the longer (3.75-inch) coolant bypass hose between the cylinder head and the water pump. Also, the 1×3/4×5/8-inch-thick cast rectangle at the top of the deck had a 1.5-inch

space between it and the water pump's mounting flange.

The BH-type blocks that have extra ribs on the water jacket side of the block were produced as part of this production series of 225 RGFC engines.

225-ci RG (1976–1991)

The last major cylinder block type produced was the high-deck (RG) cast-iron block with the nodular cast-iron crankshaft (RGCC). These RGCC blocks were produced from the middle of 1976-model production through the end of the Slant Six production run. Most carried engine block casting number 330 or 530 on the driver's side of the block.

RGCC blocks had five freeze plugs at the same height and the same coolant bypass hose and cast-in rectangle spacing as noted above. Cast-crank SL6 engines have the capital letter "E" stamped into the ID pad, after the displacement number (225E). The easy-to-spot feature for the RGCC engine block was the thickness of the cast-in gusset behind the water pump's mounting flange. On cast-iron crankshaft engine blocks, this gusset is a uniform 5/16 inch, straight across the back of the water pump flange. This gusset tapers from 3/8 inch up to 3/4-inch thickness on all forged crankshaft Slant Six engine blocks, with the only exception being the 1976 "030" RGFC block casting.

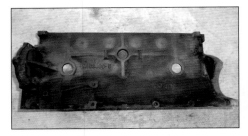

The driver's side of an early raised-block 225 with three freeze plugs has casting number 2463430. The center freeze plug is located higher than the outer two, and the gusset behind the water pump is tapered. All these blocks came with a forged-steel crankshaft.

The later-raised Slant Six engine block has five freeze plugs and came with forged-steel or cast-iron crankshafts. The forged-steel crankshaft block carries casting number 2806830 and was also used to build 198-ci Slant Six engines.

225-ci Aluminum

The die-cast aluminum-block 225 Slant Six had a high deck and used the forged-steel crankshaft (ALFC). The aluminum-block Slant Six is different from all the other cast-iron block engines. There were 50,000 engines produced from 1961 to early 1963 model years, using a state-of-the-art high-pressure die-casting process.

The aluminum block had cast-in-place iron cylinder sleeves, used two-piece (top and bottom) cast-iron main cap inserts with longer main cap bolts, and did not use cam bearing inserts (the camshaft journals rode directly on the aluminum block).

Looking at the coolant bypass hose is the fastest way to see if the engine is a low-block 170 or a tall-block 225 or 198. The tall block has the 3.5-inch-long hose as shown; low-block engines have about a 1.5-inch hose.

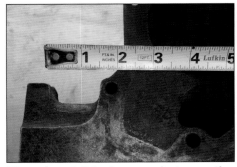

There is a 1.5-inch space between the water pump's mounting flange and the rectangular casting lump on 225 and 198 engine blocks.

The aluminum block had an open-top deck design with the head gasket's fire ring sealing on the tops of the freestanding cast-iron cylinder bore sleeves. Longer and deeper threaded head bolt holes and longer head bolts are used to get the needed clamping force on the head gasket. The aluminum block carried casting number 2121355 on the driver's side, and a magnet will not stick to this block.

The fastest way to identify one of the rare Slant Six aluminum blocks is to look for freeze plugs. All of the cast-iron Slant Six engine blocks had freeze plugs along the driver's side of

The tapered horizontal rib or gusset behind the water pump mounting indicates that this block has a forged-steel crankshaft. "BH" blocks have two extra pencil-shaped ribs running top to bottom, in front and behind the row of freeze plugs.

BH engine blocks have extra ribs in front and behind the row of five freeze plugs. In general, the 1968–1975 RGFC blocks show higher casting quality compared to the earlier three–freeze plug block with the BH blocks being sought after for high-performance and race engine buildups.

The thinner and straight horizontal rib, or gusset, behind the water pump mounting flange indicates that this five–freeze plug RG engine block has a nodular cast-iron crankshaft.

the block, but the aluminum-block engine had no freeze plugs. The aluminum Slant Six was approximately 75 pounds lighter, but it was not nearly as strong as its cast-iron siblings. It is more difficult to rebuild as well. For these reasons, we will focus our attention on the more commonly found "bulletproof" cast-iron Slant Sixes.

Casting Numbers

Most Chrysler casting numbers of this era are seven digits long followed by a dash number. The number after the dash identifies the casting pattern equipment used to mold a specific part. There are also some letters and other markings that identify the foundry that made the casting and the shift that produced it. These markings include the numbers 1, 2, and 3; "D" for the day shift; and "N" for the night shift.

The Slant Six engine block casting numbers can identify a range of production years. They also identify the crankshaft type: forged steel or cast iron. The engine size, manufacturing year, and date code are also

The die-cast aluminum Slant Six engine block has its casting number on a small medallion on the manifold side of the block. The last three numbers on this block casting are less defined than the "2121" that proceeds them.

stamped into a pad, which we will discuss in detail later in this book.

VIN Stamping

The vehicle identification number (VIN) was stamped onto the Slant Six engine block starting in 1968. The VIN (or part of it) is stamped into a machined pad on the passenger's side along the lifter gallery toward the rear of the block. This pad is facing the fenderwell, so it is hard to read when the engine is installed. Use a mirror or view it from underneath the vehicle.

All forged-steel Slant Six crankshafts use the same crankshaft bearing inserts, so any forged-steel Slant Six crankshaft will fit into any Slant Six engine block made for a forged-steel crank. The only exception to this rule is trying to install a long-stroke 225 crankshaft into a short-stroke 170 engine block. The longer throws on the 225 crankshaft interfere with the smaller crankshaft pocket area found in the 170 engine block.

Likewise, any cast-iron Slant Six crankshaft will swap into any cast crank Slant Six engine block. This is

The early engine block stampings have a letter to define the year and the first two numbers of the displacement followed by a build sequence code. "V22" indicates a 225-ci 1964-model engine.

important because a lightweight cast crank was offered late in the Slant Six production run (1984 to the end of production). A fast way to identify a cast crankshaft Slant Six engine block is to look at the gusset thickness on the back of the water pump's mounting flange or inspect the crankshaft or its bearings.

Decoding Engine Block ID Stampings

By Daniel Stern (aka SlantSixDan)

Identifying a Slant Six engine (or engine block) requires finding and understanding the block casting number and the engine ID code. The ID code was stamped on the block at the final stage of manufacture. These "what, when, and where" block stamping numbers will indicate some or all of the following:

- Vehicle model year the engine was originally built for
- Cubic inch displacement of the engine
- Whether the engine was built for a car or truck/van
- Where the engine was built (production plant)
- Engine build date (month and day)
- Gasoline type the engine was designed to run on (regular or premium)
- Nonstandard-size parts in the engine (if any)

The stamping code format changed over the years, and there are some "gotchas" in the system. The assembly plants sometimes deviated from the official Chrysler Corporation format, and it's not uncommon to find carelessly or improperly stamped engines. Decoding the stamping, piece by piece, even in accord with the correct-year parts and service manuals, won't necessarily tell you what you're looking at. You'll sometimes have to use other clues to confirm or correct what the stamping says.

Where's the Code?

To decode the stamping, you have to find it. On most Slant Six engines, it's on a 1/4-inch protruding ledge of the deck surface located on the distributor side of the block, outboard of the front (number-1) cylinder, and facing the sky. This puts the stamping below the front spark plug on an assembled engine, behind and below the alternator, inboard of the ignition coil, in the most common Slant Six engine configuration. This ledge usually gets crudded up with grease and dirt over the years, so you may have to scrape and wipe the area clean to reveal the stamping.

Exceptions are first-year (1960) engines that are stamped elsewhere, often in a similar location but at the rear instead of at the front or behind the water pump. Late-production engines (1980s) may also be stamped on the passenger-side edge near the rear cylinder.

First in the stamping sequence is the vehicle model year that the engine was originally built for. Through 1973, this was encoded with a letter, as shown on page 23.

The letters aren't fully sequential; we jump from V for 1964 to A for 1965, and the letters U and I are not used. The letter Q is also not used in engine stampings, which is a bit of a "gotcha" because these year letters were also used to designate the cars themselves ("R series" for 1961, "S series" for 1962, etc.). For some reason, Chrysler designated all 1960 models as P-series cars except the 1960 Valiant, which it called a Q-series, yet 1960 Valiant engines have P-code date stamps.

Starting in 1974, the letter identification system went away, and the last digit of the model year was used instead: 4 for 1974, 5 for 1975, 6 for 1976, and so on. By the early 1980s, Chrysler Corporation was a disorganized mess, and the chaos even extended to engine stampings. Some plants carried on using the last digit of the model year, while others used letters of one kind or another. Fortunately, by that time there were usually other clues to help sort out

what you're looking at. Sometimes it's unclear until you cross-reference the stamping with the block's casting number (or lack of numbers) to narrow down the range of possibility.

Displacement Stamping

After the model year comes the engine displacement, or "what" number(s). Only the first two digits of the displacement were used through 1964, so 17 for a 170-ci engine or 22 for a 225. Starting in 1965, the entire displacement was stamped: 170 or 225 through 1969, 198 or 225 from 1970 to 1974, and just 225 starting in 1975.

Before we get to the when-and-where part of the stamping, we need to consider some additional gotcha points, in the form of extra letters and letters that mean more than one thing. From 1961 to 1963, Chrysler built about 50,000 aluminum-block 225 engines. These had an A (for aluminum) after the model year in the stamping, so RA 22 for a 1961 engine, SA 22 for a 1962, and TA 22 for a 1963 aluminum-block Slant Six. The letter A also means 1965, and T also means a truck engine, so TA 22 means a 1963 aluminum 225 passenger-car engine,

Starting in 1968, the VIN legally had to be stamped into the engine block. The Slant Six used a machined pad located at the rear of the lifter gallery rail.

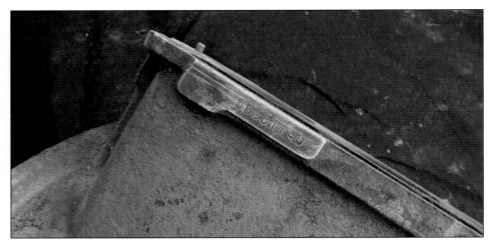

A close-up view of a vehicle identification number (VIN). If this is your vehicle's VIN number, I have the original Slant Six engine block out of it!

The Slant Six engine manufacturing information stamping is commonly found on the passenger's side of the block, under the number-1 spark plug.

but AT 225 means an iron-block 225 built for a 1965-model truck.

The when and where parts of the stamping come next. Two different systems were used for indicating when the engine was assembled. Starting in 1960, it was a simple month-day stamping: 8 2 means August 2; 10 17 means October 17; 5 5 means May 5; and so on. Here's another gotcha point: remember we're talking about model years, not calendar years. The

Model Year Stamping Codes	
Model Year	*Code*
1960	P
1961	R
1962	S
1963	T
1964	V
1965	A
1966	B
1967	C
1968	D
1969	E
1970	F
1971	G
1972	H
1973	J

changeover from the current model to the next year's model was in September, so take care to decode the month and day correctly, in accord with the letter indicating the model year: a month indicator of 9, 10, 11, or 12 means September, October, November, or December of the calendar year before the indicated model year.

This is where most pre-1968 engine stampings stop providing useful information. Extra numbers such as -2 or -3 were internal production line or shift codes that were used at the factory for keeping track of which engines came off which line. They aren't meaningful for engine identification in the field.

Let's look at a few samples of early engine stampings:

Q 17 7 13 is a 1960 Valiant 170 engine assembled on July 13, 1960.
P 22 10 4 is a 1960 Plymouth/ Dodge 225 engine assembled on October 4, 1959 (model year!).
S 22 6 12 is a 1962 iron-block 225 engine assembled on June 12, 1962.
SA 22 6 12 is a 1962 aluminum-

block 225 engine assembled on June 12, 1962.
V 17 11 17 is a 1964 170 engine assembled on November 17, 1963 (model year!).
B 225 3 7 is a 1966 225 engine assembled on March 7, 1966.
TA 22 4 9 is a 1963 aluminum-block 225 engine assembled on April 9, 1963.
AT 225 4 9 is a 1965 225 truck engine assembled on April 9, 1965.

Now for more "gotcha" points: With this system it's easy to have what looks like a stamping that conflicts with itself. For example, how about A 170 2 25? That's got both "170" and "225" in it, and due to random spacing it's entirely possible it would appear as A 170 225, but remember the stamping code order of year, displacement, date to figure out that this is a 1965 170 engine assembled on February 25, 1965.

10,000-Day Calendar

Chrysler started using a 10,000-day calendar on July 29, 1961. That date was indicated by a code of 0001. The following day (July 30, 1961) was 0002, and so on. It's easy to find a decoder for this calendar by doing an Internet search for "Chrysler 10,000 day calendar." You can then enter a code and find out what date it means.

The gotcha is this kind of date code was applied on engines starting for the 1968 model year, but some plants switched over several years earlier, and some plants hung on to the old way for quite a few years. If you see an engine stamped V 22 10 92, that's a sure sign you're looking at the new-type date code rather than an old-type code because there's no such date as October 92. Put *1092* into an online decoder and it tells you that means July 24, 1964.

But what if you're faced with V 22 11 07? A plain reading gives November 7, 1963 (remember we're talking about model years), which is valid. Plugging it in the online 10,000-day calendar gives August 8, 1964, which is an equally valid date. In a case like this, you'll have to either use other clues, such as the build date of the engine's original vehicle if you can find it out, or let it remain a somewhat mysterious 1964 engine.

Engine Plant Stamping 1968 and Beyond

Officially there was no provision for the "where" in 1967 or earlier engine stampings; the engine plant wasn't indicated. Starting in 1968, the engine plant was sometimes indicated with T or PT for Trenton, Michigan; M or PM for Mound Road, Michigan; and W or PW for Windsor, Canada. Alternatively, sometimes engines built at the Windsor engine plant had a C prefix. And look, it's that pesky letter T again, which now has *three* meanings to keep track of: 1963 model year, truck engine, and Trenton engine plant. Later on, K or PK was added to mean the engine plant at Toluca, Mexico.

In addition, in the middle of the 1976 model year the crankshaft on the Slant Six was changed from forged steel to cast iron, as detailed elsewhere in this book. Cast-crank engines have an E in their stamping, adding a second meaning to that letter besides 1969.

Here are some sample stampings that might be found on engines made for 1968 or later passenger cars and trucks:

3W225 4326 decodes as follows:

3 = 1973 model year
W = Windsor engine plant
225 = Engine displacement
43 26 = June 1, 1973
(on the 10,000-day calendar)

CG198 3434 decodes as follows:
C = Windsor engine plant
(C for Canada)
G = 1971 model year
198 = Engine displacement
3434 = December 22, 1970
(on the 10,000-day calendar)

F225R 7 6 decodes as follows:
F = 1970 model year
225 = Engine displacement
R = Regular-fuel engine
7 6 = July 6, 1970
(old-style date stamp)

E225T 2789 contains a gotcha:
E = 1969 model year
225 = Engine displacement
T = Truck engine *or*
Trenton engine plant (gotcha!)
2789 = March 17, 1969
(on the 10,000-day calendar)

7M225E 5555 decodes as follows:
7 = 1977 model year
M = Mound Road engine plant
225 = Engine displacement
E = Cast-iron crankshaft
5555 = October 12, 1976
(on the 10,000-day calendar)

As the 1970s and 1980s progressed, some engine plants seemed to drift randomly between using month-day dates and using date codes from the 10,000-day calendar. You might find production line/shift codes of up to four digits before or after the date code. It's best to think about all the possible meanings of the stamped number you are reviewing, including the results of putting any four-digit codes into the online 10,000-day calendar. With that information, it's usually possible to discard the meanings that don't make sense and narrow in on the correct identification for the engine you're looking at.

ID Stamping

The ID stamping location was also used for additional indicator markings. For a time in the 1960s and 1970s, there were three ruggedness levels of the Slant Six engine in trucks and vans: the 225-1 was similar to the passenger-car engine, the 225-2 had some heavy-duty parts, and the 225-3 had even more heavy-duty parts. If you find an engine stamped 225-1, 225-2, or 225-3, that's what it refers to.

Although all Slant Six engines were built to run on regular gasoline, Chrysler sometimes stamped engines (6- and 8-cylinder alike) configured for regular gasoline *or* built for passenger car usage with R. This added a second and third meaning to that letter besides 1961. Passenger car engines could also be indicated by PC, while premium-fuel engines could be indicated with P (adding a second meaning to P besides 1960, except for the Valiant).

After the what-when-where information, there will sometimes be a how. If the engine was originally built with nonstandard-size parts, that will be indicated (at least in theory) with characters in the stamping. For instance, an engine originally built with oversize tappets may have a diamond symbol. An engine built with one or more 0.001-inch undersize main or connecting rod bearings is supposed to be indicated by a Maltese cross symbol in the engine stamping (another stamping on the crankshaft

An example of a Maltese cross is shown on this identification pad stamping. Can you decode the rest of the information?

tells which one), and a Maltese cross followed by an X indicates the engine was built with all 0.010-inch undersize rod and/or main bearings. Similarly, A can mean one or more oversize cylinder bores (another meaning besides 1965), and X can mean nonstandard valve guides (another meaning besides the one that goes with the Maltese cross). This isn't likely to be useful information many years after the engine was first built because any rebuild will involve careful measurement to determine the right bearing sizes, valve guides, and cylinder bores.

Random Markings and Stampings

Other markings sometimes found on 1980s engines include HP for a high-performance version and S for an undefined "special" version. Another marking seldom seen on engines built in the United States, Canada, Australia, or South Africa is LC, which indicates the engine was built with low-compression pistons. Those engines were exported to countries where the gasoline had a very low octane rating.

There are some other possibilities for what you might find on the engine ID pad. Numbers that make no sense in terms of the systems described here might be a partial VIN, a date that doesn't comport with anything else about the engine, or numbers that look random. You might find all or part of the words SERVICE or WARRANTY. These are usually cases where an engine was replaced by a dealer service department, especially if it happened under warranty. You may find the stamping pad completely blank. This can also indicate a replacement engine because new engines and blocks came from Chrysler with nothing stamped on the pad, or it can mean the original stamping has been obliterated by block deck resurfacing or during a car theft (thieves would sometimes weld up and reface the stamping pad to thwart identification of stolen vehicles).

Factory Engine Paint

If all else fails and you're stuck trying to identify an engine with an absent, illegible, or nonsensical stamping, you can sometimes gain a bit of insight if you can figure out what color the engine was originally painted. It's not a sure thing, but it can be helpful if it's all you have. Here's a guide:

Metallic dark turquoise: 225 engines in 1960–1961 Plymouth and Dodge cars, North American market

Silver: 225 engines in some 1961 Valiant and Lancer cars in the US market, and RV1-series 1962 Valiants in Australia

Red: All 1962–1968 170 and 225 engines in passenger cars in all markets except as below, plus 170 engines in all 1960 and most 1961 Valiant/Lancer cars and 1961–1962 trucks in the US market

Light turquoise: 170 and 225 engines in 1969 passenger cars and trucks in the US market, 170 engines in 1962–1966 Canadian-built Valiants, and 1967–1969 225 engines with 2-barrel carburetion in the Australian market

Blue: 198 and 225 engines in 1970–1983 passenger cars and trucks in the North American market

Orange: 1967 and up 225 engines with 2-barrel carburetion, South African market

Yellow: 225 engines in 1962–1968 trucks/vans/buses, North American market

Black: 1984 and up 225 engines in all applications, North American market

The information presented here applies to engines built for the US market. It also applies to Canadian-market engines starting in 1966 when the Auto Pact integrated the US and Canadian markets for vehicles and parts. Markings on pre-1966 Canadian engines and on Australian, Mexican, Turkish, South African, Spanish, and Swiss engines are likely to differ from what is described here. No matter what country you're in, if you're faced with a block stamping that defies decoding with this information, ask an expert. As this book goes to print, most of the world's Slant Six owners and experts can be found on the Internet, in the forums at slantsix.org and others based in Australia, South Africa, Spain, Mexico, and elsewhere around the world.

ENGINE TUNING, EVALUATION, AND DIAGNOSIS

The Chrysler Slant Six is a well-designed engine that can take lots of hard use, so you want to carefully evaluate any engine before taking it apart for rebuilding. Evaluation of a nonrunning engine is limited. You should do everything possible to get the engine running. If the engine is already out of the vehicle and still assembled, check the following:

- Was the engine stored indoors, kept well covered, and kept dry?
- Are there any obvious cracks or physical damage, such as a damaged oil pan, damaged valve cover, bent flex plate, broken casting ears, stripped bolt hole(s), or rusty water drip marks?

- Is the motor oil still inside, and is it clean? Cut open the oil filter if it is still present.
- Remove the spark plugs. Are any of the spark plug tips damaged or rusty?
- Attempt to turn the engine over with a wrench. Does it turn over freely?

Finding any of the listed issues makes a "good running engine" suspect. Any loose engine you find that is seized up, shows a lot of metal in the oil filter, or has physical damage

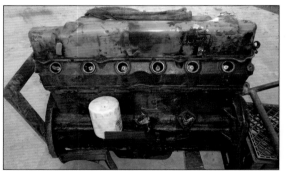

The passenger's side of the engine shows that the oil filter and distributor's splash shield are still attached. The engine's build number stamping is present, and we see the original factory embossed steel head gasket, which indicates that this engine has never been disassembled.

This engine is mostly complete and turns over with a wrench. It has rags plugging the openings and was kept dry, so it looks like a pretty good core for rebuilding.

The Slant Six vibration damper is a press fit, so there is no large center bolt present. Install a 3/8-16 hex-head bolt in one of the outer tapped damper holes if you need a way to rotate the engine with a wrench.

This engine core had green coolant running out of it, which is a good indication that the cooling system was maintained. Engines that were run for long periods on water alone will need additional water jacket cleaning.

Tech Tip

Check the fuel quality before attempting to start any vehicle that has not run in more than 90 days. Gasoline absorbs moisture and goes bad (turns into varnish) over time. If in doubt, drain and refill the gas tank or connect a separate gas can so you run the engine on good fuel. ∎

Tech Tip

Remove the fan belts and momentarily run the engine to test for accessory noises. ∎

does not qualify as a good core for rebuilding. Try to avoid these. Skip forward to the engine inspection chapter if the engine you find has already been disassembled.

There are many additional checks and tests that can be done to a running engine. Try to get the engine to run, especially if it is still in a vehicle. If the engine will not turn over or run, perform the checks at the beginning of this chapter to get some idea of whether it is a candidate for rebuilding. If the engine runs, check the following:

- Will the engine stay running at lower RPM?
- Do you have oil pressure? Does the engine overheat at idle?
- Does the engine miss, run roughly, or backfire?
- Is there excessive smoke? If so, what color (white, black, blue)?
- Are there oil, fuel, or water leaks?
- Do you hear any loud noises? If so, in what area of the engine (up high or lower down)?

If a Slant Six engine stays running, has oil pressure, does not make loud knocking noises, and does not quickly overheat at idle, you should fix any obvious leaks or problems. The next step in the evaluation process is to pull off the valve cover to check and adjust the valve clearances.

If the engine runs fine but has excessive blue tailpipe smoke, oil consumption, bad oil leakage, or loud knocking noises, check the following items before deciding to pull the engine for rebuilding:

Excessive blue tailpipe smoke:
- Is the crankcase oil level too high? Check to see if the dipstick is the correct length.
- Does the engine have a clogged or incorrect PCV valve?
- Is the incorrect carburetor base to intake manifold gasket installed?
- Is the carburetor base gasket reversed and blocking the PCV port?
- Is the intake manifold PCV port or hose clogged?

Excessive black tailpipe smoke:
- Does the engine have a misadjusted or sticking choke?
- Does it have a misadjusted or malfunctioning carburetor?

- Is the PCV valve clogged or incorrect?
- Has excessive fuel diluted into the engine oil?

High oil consumption:
- Is the crankcase oil level too high?
- Is the PCV valve clogged or incorrect?
- Is the oil pressure sending unit leaking?
- Are there plugged or sticky piston oil control rings?

Excess oil leakage:
- Is the crankcase oil level too high?
- Is the oil pressure sending unit leaking?
- Have old or split spark plug tube O-rings and/or damaged spark plug tubes been changed?
- Are the oil pan or valve cover bolts loose?
- Is the oil pan drain plug loose?

Loud knocking noises:
- Are there any loose torque converter flex plate bolts (automatic transmission only)?
- Are there any worn or failing accessories (water pump, alternator, power steering, or fuel pump)?

Mechanical Lifter Valve Lash

Slant Six engines produced until 1981 used solid lifters and adjustable rocker arms to open and close the valves. There is a small amount of clearance, called lash, designed into this system, and those settings (different clearances for intake valves versus exhaust valves) must be initially set and then periodically checked and adjusted during the life of the engine.

Correct valve lash adjustment ensures smooth, quiet, and trouble-free operation. Valve seat recession will reduce valve lash clearance and engine performance declines. The valvetrain becomes noisy as the valve clearances become wider with wear. If the lash is insufficient, the engine misses or the idle becomes rough, and you risk burning the exhaust valves.

The valve lash clearances are crucial to solid lifter engine performance and smooth operation, so it is the first thing that should be checked and adjusted when troubleshooting or tuning a pre-1981 Slant Six. The job of lashing valves sounds intimidating, especially to the novice mechanic, but it is a straightforward process that uses common hand tools. It can easily be performed in a couple of hours. The end results will be:

- Improved engine performance and economy
- Smooth idle and better throttle response
- Quiet valvetrain operation
- Improved engine vacuum readings
- Less chance of burning an exhaust valve or ejecting a pushrod

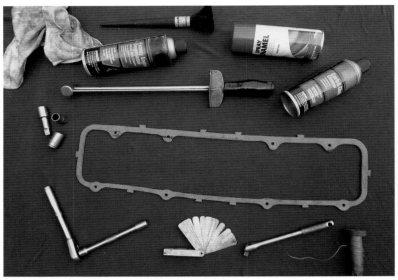

The tools needed for a valve adjustment include 3/8, 7/16, 9/16, 11/16 sockets and a torque wrench. A thickness gauge set ("feeler gauges") is the only specialty tool required. Spray solvent, paint, rags, and some fine wire are other items that are nice to have available. Be sure to have a replacement valve cover gasket before starting the job.

Performing the lash adjustment also gives you a chance to inspect and improve other items that affect overall engine performance. It will help you decide whether the engine needs additional work. The solid lifter valve clearance adjustment activities reviewed here will do more than quiet down a ticking tappet or smooth out a rough idle. The job also includes:

- General inspection of the engine's top end. Is it clean or caked with sludge? Any broken valve springs?
- Inspect the pushrods. Have any jumped out of place? Are they all spinning as the engine runs? Are any bent?
- Inspect the valve stem seals. Are they hard and crumbly or soft and doing their jobs?
- Check cylinder head and rocker arm shaft bolt torque. Are all the bolts at the correct tightness?
- Inspect the rocker arm assembly for oiling. Is each rocker arm feeding oil to the valve and pushrod?

Tech Tip

You will need the following items and tools to do a lash adjustment on a Slant Six:
- New valve cover gasket
- Socket set
- Feeler gauges: 0.006- to 0.025-inch range minimum
- Torque wrench, ft-lb type
- Spray carburetor cleaner
- Solvent or engine cleaner
- Spray paint for the valve cover (optional) ■

- Clean and inspect the PCV valve and breather cap. Are they clogged? Are the hoses in good condition?
- Straighten and reseal the valve cover. Ensure that engine oil is not getting past the valve cover gasket.

It's best to do the lash adjustment on a hot, running engine. It can also be done on a cold, nonrunning engine. To do a running-engine

Start the valve adjustment process by removing the air filter assembly, the vacuum advance hose, the PCV valve, and the temperature sending unit wire. You may have to disconnect and move the heater hoses. Loop one of the hoses around and reconnect it to the engine so you can start and run it for the valve adjustment.

It is a good idea to put an oil drip pan or a piece of cardboard under the vehicle before removing the valve cover for the running valve adjustment. Place this protection on the passenger's side where the oil drips will land.

valve lash adjustment, run/drive the vehicle so it is at normal temperature. Place a piece of cardboard or a drip pan under the engine, if you are worried about oil drops. Remove the valve cover, disconnecting hoses and wires to get the valve cover off if necessary.

Initial Inspection and Cleaning

Inspect the rocker arms, valve spring, valve stem seals, and pushrods for obvious damage. Restart the engine. See if all the pushrods are spinning and are straight (a bent pushrod will wobble or not spin). Look at the rocker arms to see if oil is coming out of the top and the tip holes. Clean any nonoiling rocker arms and replace any bent pushrods before doing the lash adjustment.

Bolt Tightness and Retorquing

Check the cylinder head bolt tightness with a torque wrench. Since we are retorquing the head gasket, start with the center bolts and work outward, per the head gasket and bolt torque pattern. Take each bolt up to 70 ft-lbs to see if it moves. You should hear a "pop" as the bolt breaks free and starts to move, then torque to specification. Move to the next bolt if the bolt being checked does not start moving by 70 ft-lbs.

Be careful when retorquing; you do not want to break a head bolt. Take note of any bolts that require a lot of additional tightening because this could indicate a head gasket failure or a warped or cracked cylinder head. Additional cylinder head bolt torque will reduce the valve lash, so be ready to loosen the lash if the head takes a lot of additional bolt torque. Check the tightness of the rocker arm shaft bolts prior to adjusting the lash.

Valve Sequence and Clearances

The amount of valve clearance is different between the intake and the exhaust valves, so review the valve order prior to starting the engine and doing the actual adjustment. The valve sequence, front to back or back to front, is exhaust, intake, exhaust, intake, exhaust, intake, intake, exhaust, intake, exhaust, intake, exhaust. From the front of the engine, the first valve is an exhaust valve followed by an intake valve. There are two intake valves that are side by side in the center of the engine. The last valve in the line (nearest to the firewall) is an exhaust valve. Look at the intake and exhaust manifold runners to help identify which type of valve you are working with.

Slant Six engines with a stock camshaft need 0.010-inch clearance on the intake valves and 0.020-inch clearance on the exhaust valves. The exhaust valves run much hotter, which is why those need more room for expansion. When it comes to solid lifter camshaft clearances, too loose is better than too tight; keep that in mind as you do the adjustments.

Conducting a Lash Adjustment

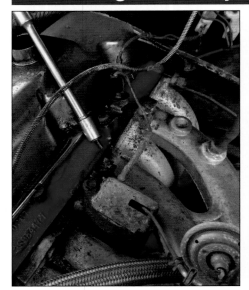

1 Remove all the valve cover bolts using a 7/16-inch socket and a 6-inch extension. Be sure all of the surrounding wires and hoses are clear before trying to remove the valve cover. You may need to give the cover a few taps with a rubber mallet if it is stuck to the gasket.

2 Slip the valve cover out from under the heater hoses and out of the engine compartment. Spray the valve cover with engine degreaser or solvent and allow it to soak while you are doing the valve adjustment.

3 The lifters are designed to spin as they pass over the cam lobes. This action also spins the pushrod, so put a mark on each of the pushrods to see if each one is spinning while the engine is running.

5 Check all of the cylinder head bolts for the correct torque. Do this check with the engine warm and follow the head gasket torque pattern, starting at the center bolts and working outward. Additional bolt tightness will affect the valve clearance, so check bolt tightness before doing the final valve lash adjustment.

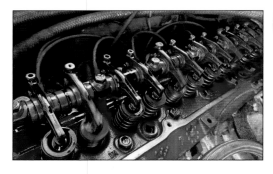

4 With the valve cover off and the engine running, inspect all of the rocker arms to see if they are oiling the valve stem and the pushrod. Oil should come out of the tip and the top of each rocker arm in equal amounts. It will take a minute or two after engine start-up for the oil to appear at each rocker arm.

6 It is also a good idea to check the rocker arm shaft retaining bolts prior to lash adjustment. Be sure those are all torqued to 30 ft-lbs.

7 Everything looked good when I pulled the valve cover off this engine. The paint overspray on the valve springs indicates that this engine had some previous work done to it. The intake and exhaust manifold runners help indicate which valves are intakes and which are exhaust.

8 *We like to use different style valve spring retainers on the intake versus the exhaust valves when rebuilding a Slant Six cylinder head. This makes the valves easier to identify during a valve lash adjustment. The flat-retainer style is used on the intake valves and the dished style is on the exhaust valves.*

9 *Flat-style feeler gauges work well for doing the lash adjustment. Do a quick check of all of the valves first and loosen any tight ones to help smooth out the idle. Continue to do the adjustment on intake and exhaust valves as groups to minimize switching off between the two different thickness gauges.*

10 *Tight exhaust valve clearance will make the engine idle poorly, so start the quick check by focusing on all the exhaust valve clearances first. Loosen any tight ones you find, then go back and do a more precise final adjustment once the engine is running smoother.*

11 *It takes some practice to use the feeler gauge and turn the adjustment screws at the same time. A socket instead of a wrench is easier to keep on the adjusting screw, but some prefer to use a small breaker bar instead of a ratchet so they do not have to keep changing the ratchet's direction.*

12 *Sometimes the engine will run better with the valve lash set a little looser than the advertised clearance settings. This is especially true with aftermarket cams, so it is a good idea to try some other clearances to decide what works best before you do the final adjustment.*

13 *The long, skinny valve cover gasket is held in place by*  *inserting gasket tabs into notches around the edge of the valve cover. Use some fine wire to hold the gasket in place while maneuvering the valve cover into position. Another option is to tie a loop of sewing thread or dental floss through each of the cover and gasket bolt holes. This is helpful if any of the gasket tabs are broken off or if the valve cover does not have notches.*

14 *The backside view of a retaining wire shows how it holds the valve cover gasket in place. Inexpensive cork valve cover gaskets will often have gasket tabs that are not aligned well with the notch in the valve cover. In that case, the tab must be removed and the gasket secured to the cover with fine wire or thread.*

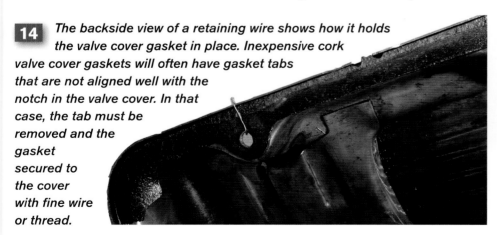

15 *Clean and reassemble the wires and hoses you removed. This engine now runs even better than it looks!*

Initial Adjustment

With tools ready, restart the engine and turn the idle speed down as low as possible. A low idle speed helps you feel the clearance and will make it easier to get your wrench on the adjustment ball screw head. A piece of heatproof tape over the PCV valve will help slow the idle way down.

Do the adjustment in two steps, starting with a quick check and then doing a fine-tune final adjustment. Slip the thickness gauge in between the rocker arm tip pad and the top of the valve stem. The first quick check pass is done to simply see if any of the valve clearances are too tight.

Starting with the exhaust valves, use a 0.018-inch gauge to see if all of the exhaust valves have at least 0.018-inch clearance. If the 0.018-inch thickness gauge does not fit in, loosen that rocker arm adjustment screw enough to let the gauge in freely (the ideal clearance for the exhaust valves is 0.020 inch, so a slightly thinner 0.018-inch gauge should go in easily).

Do the same quick check on the intake valves. The intake valves run cooler, so quick-check them with the final 0.010-inch gauge. Just make sure all the intake valves have at least 0.010-inch clearance. The engine may smooth out and idle faster once you have the minimum clearance on all the valves, so turn the idle down more if you can before doing the final check and adjustment. I recommend doing all of the intake valves and then all the exhaust valves, so you do not have to keep switching gauges as you go down the row of valves.

Final Adjustment of the Intake Valves

Stay on the intake valves and do the final adjustment to a 0.010-inch clearance. The clearance on those valves is already at 0.010 inch or more, based on loosening you may have done during the quick check. Now you will want to tighten any clearances that are overly loose.

The clearance is correct when the 0.010-inch gauge fits into the space with a slight amount of drag. This is where you need to develop an experienced "touch" or "feel" by using slightly thinner and thicker gauges to test with. For the intake valves, that would look like this: a 0.008-inch gauge would fly right into the gap, a 0.009-inch gauge would easily go in, a 0.011-inch gauge would be a tight fit, and a 0.012-inch gauge would almost completely refuse to go in.

Pay attention to the sounds the running engine makes during adjustment. Overly loose valve clearance will be accompanied by a ticking sound, while tight clearance creates a misfire and a rough idle.

Final Adjustment for the Exhaust Valves

The exhaust valves are the most sensitive to heat expansion, so do their final adjustment after the engine has been running at temperature for a while. Proceed the same way as you did with the intake valve clearances, using a range of gauge sizes (0.018-, 0.019-, 0.021-, and 0.022-inch gauges) to feel for the correct clearance setting. Turn the adjustment screw and listen to the engine for ticking or missing noises.

I like to adjust the exhaust valve clearances on the looser side of the specification for smoother idle and reduced chance of burning an exhaust valve. You may want to try 0.021 inch or 0.022 inch of clearance to see how you like it. Again, when in doubt, stay to the loose side when it comes to setting valve lash clearances on solid lifter cams.

Make a final pass through all the valves once they have all been adjusted. You should hear a slight engine miss as you insert the gauge under each rocker arm tip (because the gauge is artificially taking up/zeroing out the lash clearance). You have done a good adjustment job if the miss you hear is pretty even, cylinder to cylinder, as you run down the row.

Once you are satisfied with the adjustment, wipe everything down and reinstall the valve cover and anything else you may have disconnected. Pay close attention to the temperature sending unit wire because it can get pinched under the valve cover gasket during reassembly.

Clearance Settings

The clearances we noted for lash adjustment are common for most factory Chrysler Slant Six solid lifter camshafts. Aftermarket or high-performance specialty cam grinds may use different valve clearance specifications. Refer to the cam grinder's recommended lash settings as a starting point, but you may want to try some variations to maximize performance and minimize valve-train noise. Said another way, valve lash settings for a particular cam may be unknown or incorrect, so do not be afraid to experiment by loosening the lash to the point of getting ticking sounds, then tightening back down by a few thousandths.

Nonrunning Valve Adjustment

The best way to set valve clearances on a nonrunning engine is by using the exhaust opening

Use a crayon or chalk to temporarily mark the rocker arms as you set the lash on each one. Marking the arms will reduce the amount of engine turning you will have to do with a wrench.

intake closing (EOIC) method. Turn the engine while watching the valve pair for one cylinder. The Slant Six valve pair layout is: exhaust, intake, exhaust, intake, exhaust, intake, intake, exhaust, intake, exhaust, intake, exhaust. There are two intake valves for different cylinders that are side by side in the center of the engine.

Adjust the intake valve of the pair when the exhaust valve of the pair is starting to open. Adjust the exhaust valve of the pair when the intake valve is fully open and starting to close. Mark the rocker arm or valve spring retainer after you adjust the valve and then turn over the engine more, watching for other valves to come into the correct adjustment position. Repeat this adjust-mark-turn engine process until all the valves have been adjusted and marked.

This method is useful for checking valve lash clearances on an engine that won't start and has little to no compression or for a newly built engine on an engine stand. You should always recheck the lash adjustment once the engine is running and warm.

Tech Tip

The Slant Six was changed from a solid lifter camshaft to a hydraulic camshaft and lifter design in 1981. Besides the different camshaft and lifters, the hydraulic lifter valvetrain has nonadjustable rocker arms, different pushrods, and a wider valve cover that requires a different valve cover gasket. The wider hydraulic lifter valve cover and gasket has an angled lower front corner. ■

Hydraulic Lifters

Hydraulic lifter preload is carefully set at the factory with more attention given to making all the valve stem heights uniform. Valvetrain wear, valve seat recession, a sloppy valve job, a head gasket thickness change, or head or cylinder block milling for increased compression can impact the hydraulic lifter preloads. Measure carefully and adjust the valve stem heights, as needed, to maintain the correct lifter preloads on a hydraulic lifter engine.

Ignition System and Valve Timing Checks

A basic engine tune-up is a well-published process, so we will not review how to change spark plugs, wires, points, condenser, or distributor cap on a Slant Six. We will review some Slant Six–specific ignition system details that can help troubleshoot problems and/or improve performance. The following engine troubleshooting information is based on checking and confirming that a solid lifter Slant Six has the correct valve lash clearance settings, which was done as the first step in the tune-up process.

If the engine cranks but will not start, test for spark at the spark plugs. This can be done by removing a spark plug wire from the plug, holding the end close to a good ground, and cranking the engine. If there is no sparking from the wire, remove the distributor cap and see if the rotor is turning when the engine is cranked. If the rotor does not turn, it is likely that the distributor's plastic drive gear is broken where it meshes with the camshaft.

With the distributor cap off, it is a good time to check for a worn timing chain and gears. Use the fan and belt (or a bolt in the front of the crankshaft) to rotate the engine forward and backward while watching the distributor's rotor. The rotor should move to the engine's turning motion, with less than 5 degrees of lost motion as you change the direction of rotation.

For an engine that cranks and seems to start but then stalls when the key is released to the *run* position, test for a bad ballast resistor, which is located on the firewall or inner fenderwell. The ballast resistor does not need to be grounded, so it is easy to plug in a replacement unit as a test. The ballast resistor can be tested with an ohm meter, and it should show 1.2 ohms of resistance when checked across the two terminals with all the wires disconnected.

If the engine runs but has a consistent misfire, pull off the coil wire and crank the engine while listening to the starter motor. You should hear a consistent rhythm as each cylinder hits compression against the starter. If you hear an uneven rhythm with inconsistency in the cranking sound, there is at least one cylinder with low or no compression. If the engine cranks consistently and runs, try

We installed a known good ballast resistor in place of the original to test a "start-and-stall" problem. This item does not need grounding, so it is easy to plug a different resistor into the circuit to test it.

The aluminum spark plug tubes on a Slant Six are a common leak point. The O-ring seals should be replaced whenever the spark plugs are removed. This engine shows two rubber O-rings stacked together, bending the base of the tubes.

the replacement spark plug and combining it with the spark plug tube adds thickness, which means the new plug's tip does not extend fully into the combustion chamber.

The reduced spark plug tip protrusion makes the plug act as if it has a colder heat range. This double gasket thickness and less plug protrusion also leaves the bottom of the spark plug's threaded hole exposed to the combustion process inside the cylinder. This allows carbon to build up in the last couple of thread turns and can make correct spark plug installation (without a ring gasket) difficult, as the plug stops turning when it hits the carbon-packed threads.

pulling off the spark plug wires, one at a time, while the engine is idling to see how it changes the idle speed and misfiring sound. If there is little to no change in the engine smoothness and sound when a particular spark plug wire is pulled off, remove and inspect that spark plug for fouling and also test the spark plug wire for continuity.

If the engine has a random misfire, check the spark timing, the spark plug wires, the spark plug heat range, and the plug tip gaps.

A common cause of misfire and oil leakage seen on 1963–1974 Slant Six heads is failure to remove the metal ring gaskets from the replacement spark plugs prior to installation. The 1960–1962 heads required the ring washers, while 1975 and later Slant Six cylinder heads were redesigned to use taper-seat spark plugs that never have gaskets.

The spark plug seats in the cylinder head were redesigned for 1963 so that the soft aluminum spark plug tube itself would serve as the plug gasket. Leaving the metal gasket on

During initial inspection of a Slant Six engine core, we noticed that the spark plug tubes were at different heights. A closer look showed that some of the tubes had two rubber O-rings stacked together. Other tubes had the original gasket, complete with factory paint overspray. These O-rings were baked rock hard and split.

The Slant Six cylinder head was redesigned in 1975 and the aluminum spark plug tubes were deleted. These heads take a different spark plug that has a tapered seat and a 5/8-inch hex, commonly called a peanut plug.

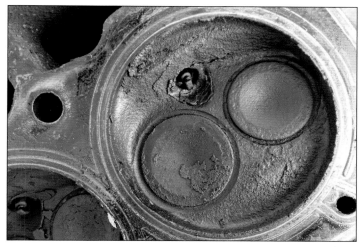

A spark plug that is not fully seated will act like a colder heat range plug and leave the last threads exposed to the combustion process. The exposed threads quickly fill with carbon, making correct spark plug installation more difficult.

The metal ring gasket was left on this plug, and then a second rubber O-ring was added to the aluminum tube. The base of the aluminum tube is now bent outward because of this improper installation.

A spark plug that does not fully seat does not pull the aluminum tube down onto the head. This means the tube's O-ring sealing gasket does not fully compress, resulting in oil leaks along the head and the passenger's side of the engine block.

Carefully check for the extra metal ring and/or spark plug gaskets when spark plugs are removed from a Slant Six. If you find the ring gaskets, remove them. To do this, grab the ring with pliers and unscrew the plug from the ring, or snip them off with wire cutters. Once they are removed, inspect the tube surfaces for distortion and check to be sure the spark plug's threaded holes are free of carbon deposits.

Reinstall the spark plugs with new rubber O-rings on the tubes. Make sure that all of the tubes compress the O-rings as the tubes are drawn down into the cylinder head and the spark plug tightens. Engine oil will leak out around the O-ring if you can wiggle the aluminum tube when the spark plug is tight.

Spark plugs to suit the pre-1975 head are available with extended projected electrodes. These seem to work especially well in most street-driven Slant Six engines. NGK spark plug number ZFR5N, stock number 3459, is a good quality example of this type of spark plug. These projected-tip plugs move the spark closer to the center of the combustion chamber for faster starts, a smoother idle, and less misfire. But they can act like a hotter heat range plug, so some timing adjustment(s) may be needed.

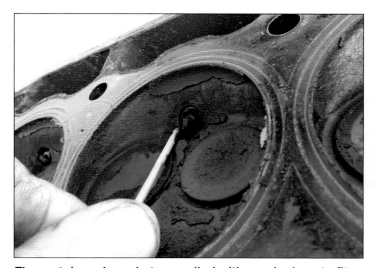

The metal crush gaskets supplied with spark plugs to fit a 1960–1974 Slant Six need to be removed if your head is a 1963–1974 unit. If not removed, the spark plug tips will not extend all the way into the combustion chamber.

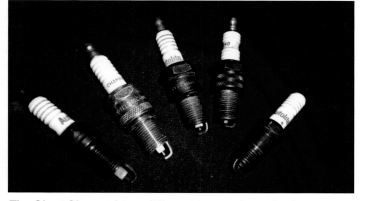

The Slant Six used two different types of spark plugs over the years. The 3/4-inch threaded reach, gasket-sealing type is used in spark plug tube heads. Heads without tubes use a spark plug with a tapered seat. There are many different heat ranges and plug tip styles available. You may want to experiment with different tip styles and/or heat ranges to see what plug works the best in your engine.

Ignition Timing

Check the ignition timing on a Slant Six by illuminating the timing mark and tab with a timing light. This should be done while the vacuum advance is disconnected and its hose is plugged. Rev the engine while checking to see if the distributor's mechanical advance system is working.

Reconnect the vacuum advance hose and check again to see if the vacuum advance system is also working. In general, a Slant Six with a stock camshaft will respond well to more initial timing advance. It will have a smoother idle and more manifold vacuum. Idle quality and manifold vacuum will start to decline as you reach 14 to 16 degrees of initial advance. For a 225 Slant Six, maximum high-RPM full-load power is made in the 28 to 30-degree total advance range. (Initial + mechanical = total timing advance.) The vacuum advance pod adds even more timing, for better off-idle response and light-load and economy driving.

All three timing advance systems can be adjusted for the best performance and economy by recurving the distributor. The practice of advancing the initial timing will likely improve idle and low-RPM performance, but doing that without recurving the distributor may also push the total timing past the preferred 30 degree maximum range. Going past that range may lead to less high-RPM power and possible detonation (pinging and preignition).

I add a second timing mark at 30 degrees advanced from the factory mark to all Slant Six dampers. This allows me to quickly check the total timing with any timing light.

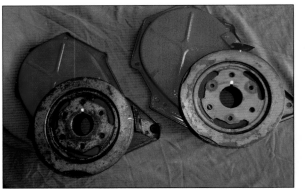

Slant Six passenger cars used two main types of timing chain covers. Early covers had a bolt-on tab, and later units had a welded-on timing tab. The position of the tab dictates the side of the vehicle the tab can be viewed from. (We prefer the welded tab, which is viewed from the distributor side of the engine.) The mark on the vibration damper is matched to the tab, so the cover, tab, and damper should always be kept together as a set. These parts are interchangeable for all engines, so mismatches can (and do) occur.

There are a few different types of timing tabs and vibration dampers used on the Slant Six. Early dampers have a bolt-on timing tab that is viewed from the manifold side of the engine, and the damper ring mark is at the four o'clock position with the keyway at twelve o'clock. Later engines have a tab welded onto the timing chain cover that is viewed from the distributor side of the engine with the mark on the damper at the one o'clock position. Check for an incorrect mix of damper and timing tab if your timing mark never comes close to the numbers on the tab.

Also, the Slant Six vibration damper consists of an inner hub and an outer ring/belt groove, bonded together with rubber. Over the years, the rubber can lose its grip, and the ring slips relative to the hub. If this happens, the timing mark is no longer accurate, even if it's the correct damper for the timing tab. For that reason, find true top dead center (TDC) by using a positive piston stop that screws into the number-1 cylinder's spark plug hole.

Camshaft Position Test

Once the factory TDC mark and tab are confirmed accurate, you can check the timing chain and gears for correct installation and/or a jumped tooth. Do this by removing the valve cover and checking the valve overlap event on the number-1 (front) cylinder at the rocker arms.

Both the intake and the exhaust valves should be slightly open at TDC exhaust stroke, so there should be no valve lash clearance at that point. The pushrods will not turn easily at TDC exhaust. Slowly rotate the engine backward until there is some clearance in the intake valve. You can now spin the intake valve's pushrod. Mark that place on the damper ring with chalk. Now rotate the engine forward until you have some lash clearance on the exhaust valve and mark that position on the damper.

The camshaft position is okay if the factory TDC mark is somewhat centered between the two new marks you just made. The cam is retarded if the first mark made (using the intake valve) is closer to the original factory TDC mark. The cam is advanced if the factory mark is closer to the second mark you made (using the exhaust valve). This test is influenced by the valve clearance settings (lash) and by "dual pattern" camshaft grinds (intake and exhaust lobes not identical). Do not panic if TDC is not exactly centered between your new marks, but do more checking if things are way off-center or way over to the retarded cam position side.

Oil Pressure and Compression Testing

The Slant Six oil pump has an integral oil filter mounting pad and was produced in 5/8-, 7/8-, and 1-inch-thick impeller sizes. The factory used the 5/8-inch impeller in a die-cast aluminum pump housing with six mounting bolt holes for most of the production engines. Aftermarket oil pump suppliers made their pump housings out of cast iron with thicker impeller sizes. Many of the aftermarket oil pumps only have five drilled mounting bolt holes.

All of the Slant Six oil pumps are externally mounted and allow access to the pump's pressure relief valve assembly. The oil pump's relief valve assembly should be removed, inspected, deburred, and cleaned on any Slant Six engine that exhibits no or very low oil pressure.

Maximum high-RPM oil pressure can be adjusted by shimming or using a stiffer relief valve spring. Low oil pressure at hot idle or low RPM can be increased by reducing the amount of engine bearing oil clearance or by changing to a thicker impeller size oil pump. Do not increase the maximum oil pressure beyond the factory's recommended 45- to 55-psi range or change to a thicker impeller size oil pump unless you really need to increase volume. The increased load can cause oil pump to camshaft drive gear failure.

The vertical oil filter mounting found on the Slant Six can lead to oil filter drainback after engine shutdown. The result is an engine that takes longer to develop oil pressure upon restart, as the filter is refilling. To prevent this, the factory used a standpipe with a built-in check valve that was screwed into the oil filter to oil pump mounting base. Replacement oil pumps don't come with a standpipe, just a plain fitting to screw on the oil filter, so if you have a standpipe, transfer it to your new oil pump.

If your engine's oil pressure gauge or warning light indicates no pressure for more than a couple of seconds, remove the oil filter, inspect and clean the check valve, and see if that solves the problem. If not, change to a different oil filter, one that has a built-in standpipe. Wix 51806 and NAPA Gold 1806 are examples of this type of filter.

Compression Check

A compression check should be performed on an engine that still runs rough after a valve lash clearance adjustment has been done. The engine should be hot and the battery should be fully charged. Remove all of the spark plugs and block the throttle open when doing a cranking compression check. PSI numbers can range from 100 to 180 psi.

The key to the test is how even the readings are from cylinder to cylinder. A cylinder leak down test should be the next check if compression readings vary from one another by more than 10 psi. Leak down testing can help determine where the compression problem is located and how bad it is. An engine with poor or no compression in a cylinder will need some level of disassembly or complete rebuilding, so additional testing with specialized tools may not be the best use of your time.

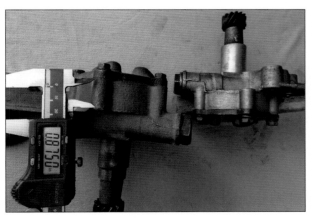

Most factory Slant Six oil pumps have a 5/8-inch-thick impeller and a die-cast aluminum housing. Aftermarket oil pumps have 7/8- and 1-inch-thick impeller sizes and cast-iron housings. The oil pressure should be 45 to 55 psi above 2,000 rpm.

The oil pump is externally mounted and allows access to the oil pressure relief valve while the engine is installed in the chassis. Remove the plug so that the spring (with the valve) can be removed for cleaning and inspection. Shimming or using a stiffer spring will increase high-RPM oil pressure, but doing this also puts more load on the delicate drive gears.

ACCESSORY AND ENGINE REMOVAL

We understand that most people reading this book are not professional mechanics or machinists, so we want to stress safety. Please be conscientious when working on automobiles and when doing engine work in particular. A Slant Six engine weighs around 450 pounds when being pulled out of a vehicle that weighs between 3,000 and 5,000 pounds, so keep this in mind as you work.

Safety First

Use the proper equipment to lift, support, move, and hold up a vehicle, as well as the engine and the parts that are attached to it. Think about what you are about to do and how you could get hurt when doing that task, then take measures to reduce the risks.

Avoid working alone, especially when moving or working around anything heavy or flammable. Do not be afraid to ask for help and to involve others in your engine rebuilding project. A second set of eyes may see something that you did not. Do not hurry or try to use brute force on something. It is better to wait, think, and ask or to approach the situation differently instead of getting hurt or damaging things.

Always use safety stands when you get under a vehicle. Work on a hard, flat surface when jacking, lifting, or moving anything heavy. Have a fire extinguisher in every work area. Ask for help or subcontract the work to a professional if you are unsure, are uncomfortable, or "get stuck" while doing a task. Bottom line: Involve others, use good judgment and common sense, and think "Safety First"!

Getting Started

Let's begin the engine removal process while leaving the transmission in the vehicle. It is a good practice to disconnect the battery before getting started. Do all of the work under the vehicle first. This will allow you to lower it back to the ground for the remainder of the engine removal process. Remove most of the difficult items at this time, such as the flex plate bolts, engine mount nuts, most of the engine to transmission bellhousing bolts, etc., making the disassembly job easier as you go.

Engine to Transmission and Chassis Attachments

Jack up the vehicle and support it safely with jack stands. Remove the dust cover(s) off the front of the transmission. Manual transmissions have a two-piece cover, and auto-

Remove the transmission bellhousing dust cover(s). The front cover is trapped by the driver-side engine to transmission support bracket, so those bolts must be removed to slip the cover out.

We notch the dust cover where the support bracket mounts so it will be easier to remove it in the future. The cover's thin sheet metal can be easily cut with tin snips or a disc grinder.

The flex plate bolts are tight, so you will have to somehow hold the engine from spinning as you break them loose. These bolts have a reduced head thickness, so use a good wrench that fits them well. You do not want to slip off and damage the heads of these special bolts.

matics have a single plate in front. Remove the bolts holding the driver's side of the engine to the transmission bellhousing support bracket in order to slip the front plate out from under it.

The bellhousing will remain attached to any manual transmission, and the bellhousing transmission assembly will stay in the vehicle. An automatic transmission's torque

converter will be unbolted from the flex plate, and it will remain in the front of the transmission and in the vehicle.

Remove all the lower engine to bellhousing bolts, leaving the two top bolts to hold the assembly together. The motor mount bracket and rubber cushion assemblies can remain on the engine, but you need to remove the large nuts and wash-

ers that hold the mount assemblies to the K-frame from underneath. The retaining nut and through bolt on later "spool type" engine mounts can be accessed from above.

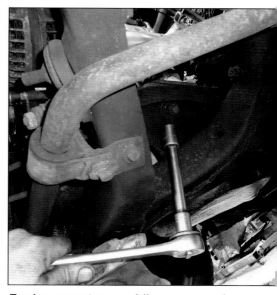

Engine mount assemblies can remain bolted to the engine, but they must be disconnected from the chassis. Access the retaining nut from underneath on most vehicles produced in the 1960s through 1972. Use a 3/4-inch socket on an extension to remove the nut.

Tech Tip

Mark the converter to flex plate relationship with spray paint. These parts only assemble one way, and it will help you later to have it clearly marked. The converter to flex plate bolts are tight and have a reduced-height hex-head for clearance; use a box wrench or socket to successfully grip the head.

The assembly will want to spin as you apply wrench force, so find a way to keep the engine from rotating as you crack the bolts loose. Our method is to use two flat-style 9/16-inch box-end wrenches to remove these bolts. We rotate the flex plate to converter assembly with one wrench so two bolt heads are accessible. Hold the rear bolt with one wrench while removing the "lead" bolt with the other wrench, based on counterclockwise rotation. Use the rear exposed bolt to rotate the assembly again so the next bolt comes into view. Hold the engine using a bolt in the front damper or by wedging a screwdriver into the assembly to hold it as you break loose and remove the last bolt. Push the torque converter rearward into the transmission after all of the flex plate bolts have been removed. ■

The right side is the same as the left. You do not have to worry about the engine dropping or shifting around when removing these nuts. The stud on the bottom of the mount will lift clear of the K-frame as the engine assembly is hoisted out of the vehicle.

The spool-type mount used on later vehicles can be accessed from above. Remove the nut and leave the through bolt in place.

Draining Fluids

Drain the engine oil and radiator coolant as the last step before lowering the vehicle. Drain fluids last to prevent lying in any spilled fluids when doing all the other undervehicle work. Once the coolant is drained, loosen the lower radiator hose clamp at the radiator and pull off the hose before putting the vehicle back on the ground.

Removing Accessories

Working from the top, disconnect and/or remove the following items from the engine:

Exhaust Pipe to Exhaust Manifold

The header pipe to exhaust manifold attaching bolts are usually rusty and the most difficult to remove, so start with those first. Earlier exhaust manifolds have a through hole here with a nut and bolt assembly holding the exhaust pipe to the manifold. Use two wrenches to loosen them. Later exhaust manifolds have threaded holes and studs, with nuts fastening

Tech Tip

Use fender protection covers or cover nicely painted surfaces with blankets to protect them while working around the engine compartment. ∎

the pipe flange to the manifold. Use penetrating oil and a tight-fitting socket or box wrench to grip the bolt and nut head. Lots of force will be needed to crack these fasteners loose.

Starter Motor

Double-check to be sure the battery is disconnected before removing the starter. Remove the wires before loosening and removing the mounting bolts. The factory often used a stud, a nut, and a split washer in the lower starter motor mounting hole to help position a dust shield that is sandwiched between the starter and transmission bellhousing. The stud, nut, washer assembly may unscrew from the bellhousing instead of the

nut loosening off the stud. If this happens, remove the stud and nut assembly, separate the parts in a vise, and reinstall the stud. Be sure to remove the dust shield, taking note of its orientation. Keep it with the starter motor.

Hoses and Radiator

Disconnect the heater hoses from the engine side only if they are in good condition and you plan to reuse them. The factory often used wire spring clamps that are best replaced with screw-type hose clamps. Put hose clamps on your shopping list, if needed.

Disconnect and remove the upper radiator hose from the engine compartment. (The lower hose should already be disconnected from the radiator.) Disconnect the transmission coolant lines (if equipped) by using two wrenches: one wrench to hold the fitting and the other wrench to turn the tube nut. Once removed, cap the lines to prevent automatic transmission fluid (ATF) drips.

Remove the radiator by loosening the lower mounting bolts a few turns and removing the top bolts completely. Pull the radiator upward until the slots at the bottom clear the mounting bolts or saddles.

Fan Belt and Fan Assembly

Crack loose the fan retaining bolt before loosening the fan belt. Then, loosen and remove the belt(s). Take note of the fan, the fan spacer (if equipped), and the pulley "stack" assembly sequence. You will need to know how to reassemble them later. Place a wrench on the fan bolt head and spin the fan to quickly unscrew each fastener.

Alternator and Upper Adjustment Bracket

Disconnect the wires and remove the slider bracket. Use two wrenches to remove the through bolt and nut assembly that mounts the alternator to its bracket. Remove the alternator and leave its mounting bracket, often with the ignition coil, connected to the engine.

Distributor Cap, Spark Plug Wires, and Distributor

Remove the distributor cap and spark plug wires. Disconnect and label any wires and hoses leading to the distributor and coil. Remove the distributor's hold-down bolt and bracket and pull the distributor out of the engine block.

Power Steering Pump (If Equipped)

Most power steering pump mounting brackets are two sections that bolt together and allow for belt adjustment. Remove the belt and split the bracket by completely removing the bracket's adjusting bolts, leaving half of the bracket on the engine and the other half on the pump. Often the pump can be "tied off" to the side of the engine compartment without disconnecting the hoses.

Air Conditioner Compressor (If Equipped)

The goal is to leave a functioning air-conditioning (AC) system connected and charged. Review the hose routing ahead of time to see if that is possible. If so, remove the AC compressor's mounting hardware from the engine and move the unit to one side. Have a professional discharge the system if hose routing does not allow for this.

Sending Unit Wires

Disconnect any oil pressure and temperature sending unit wires or mechanical gauge connections. Label the wires and move them off to the side of the engine bay.

Throttle and Kickdown Linkage

Disconnect the throttle operation cable or linkage leading to the carburetor. Take notes and photos for future reference. Then, disconnect any throttle pressure (kickdown) linkage connecting to the carburetor and remove any pieces that may interfere with engine removal. Disconnect and label any wires or hoses for electronic choke, throttle step-up solenoid, or intake air heating controls.

Other Stuff

Remove the fuel line to the fuel pump's inlet side. It is optional to remove the carburetor at this time, but we advise it.

Only disconnect and remove the things you need to in order to get the engine out of the vehicle. For example, the manifolds, motor mounts, coil, brackets, fuel pump, and water pump can all be left on the engine when a Slant Six is removed. On vehicles equipped with power steering or an air conditioner, remove the belt, disconnect the mounting, and move the unit(s) to one side of the engine compartment while leaving the hoses connected. Before starting the disassembly, spend a minute putting penetrating oil onto all the nuts and bolts that will be removed so it has time to soak in.

Engine Removal

The Slant Six has two 3/8-16 UNC threaded holes on the top of the cylinder head between the valve cover and the manifold assembly. These two holes are used to lift the engine and transmission as an assembly.

It is helpful to lubricate all the fasteners that will be removed, especially the exhaust manifold mounting studs, bolts, and nuts. Do this ahead of fastener removal so the oil has some time to soak in.

There are two 3/8-16 UNC threaded holes on the driver's side of the cylinder head. They are between the valve cover and the manifolds. Use these holes to attach a chain or a strap to lift the engine.

Only use the front tapped hole at the top of the cylinder head when lifting the engine. Remove the valve cover or use a nut or thick washer under the lift chain or strap so you do not crush the edge of the valve cover when the chain's hold-down bolt is tightened.

The factory had a special engine-lifting bracket that is bolted to these holes, but that special tool is not essential. A loop of chain or a strap can be used instead. Just be sure to not pinch the edge of the valve cover when bolting it down. Use the forward hole only when removing or installing the engine alone. Use a strap between the two holes when lifting the engine and transmission as an assembly. Using these hole(s) as described hangs the engine or engine/transmission assembly at the correct front-to-back angle and at the proper 30-degree slant.

Do a final check to be sure all necessary items have been disconnected and/or removed. Position a floor jack under the transmission to support it. Remove the last remaining bellhousing bolts and then rock the engine while lifting it to separate it from the transmission. It is helpful to lift the transmission as high as possible with the floor jack to help the engine separate and to clear the steering linkage. Continue lifting as you maneuver the engine away from the exhaust pipe(s) and other surrounding parts.

The throttle linkage rod on A-Body cars made before 1967 and the ATF cooling lines are the biggest concerns when lifting a Slant Six

engine out of the chassis. The factory metal coolant lines (tubes) swing up and under the manifold assembly, and they can get trapped by the dipstick tube. Carefully maneuver these

The Slant Six oil level dipstick came in many lengths over the years. Longer dipsticks have longer tubes that can trap the ATF coolant lines when lifting the engine. To remove the tube, use locking pliers to grip it then turn the tube side to side while pulling it up and out of the engine block.

items out of the way while lifting the engine. Tie them up and out of the way once they are clear. Long dipstick tubes should be removed prior to lifting the engine.

Removing the Engine

1 *A floor jack is used from the side of the vehicle to lift and support the transmission when removing the engine only. The jack can be rolled under the vehicle between the legs of a cherry picker and placed under the rear of the transmission when the engine and transmission are removed together.*

Raise the jack as the assembly rolls forward to get everything over the steering center link.

Removing the Engine CONTINUED

2 A cherry picker was used to remove the engine from this vehicle. A short piece of chain was attached to the forward bolt hole on the head. Make sure the lift chain and hoist do not damage surrounding parts. Remove additional items if in doubt, and keep checking as you lift the engine and the angles change.

3 The driver-side engine mount interfered with the exhaust pipe when pulling this engine, so we removed the mount from the block once the engine's weight was off of it.

4 Removing the two bolts and the mount made the space needed to lift the engine past the exhaust pipe. Continually check for clearance and hang-ups as you lift the engine out of the vehicle.

5 Vehicle hood removal is not necessary if you use a cherry picker hoist and attach a short hoist chain or strap close to the engine.

6 Lift the transmission as high as possible to improve the angle and prevent damage to linkage parts. A low-profile floor jack is needed when inserting the jack from the side of the vehicle. We used strong wire to hold the front of the transmission up once the engine was out so the vehicle could be moved without risk of the transmission falling off the jack.

ENGINE DISASSEMBLY

Complete engine disassembly is required in order to do a professional engine rebuild. The engine disassembly needs to be done in a safe and efficient way so the job can be completed quickly and without damaging anything (including yourself!).

Looking for obvious problems and taking some initial measurements is an important activity during engine disassembly, so do not rush through this operation. You or your machine shop will need some "as-is" information about the engine, and the measurements shown here can only be taken with the parts assembled. Don't skip the measurement steps!

Parts Removal

There are some parts that should be removed from the engine immediately after it has been lifted out of the engine bay. These parts include the valve cover, intake and exhaust manifold set, flex plate, motor mount assemblies, driver-side support bracket, alternator/coil bracket, and oil and fuel pumps. The items listed do not interfere with engine removal and are easier to get off once the engine is out of the vehicle and hanging on the hoist. Getting these items off the engine now will prevent damage to them and lighten the assembly.

Parts best left on the engine when it is pulled from the vehicle include the flex plate, fuel pump, water pump, alternator bracket, harmonic damper, engine mounts, and bracket assemblies. Remove these items once the engine is out of the engine compartment and you have better access.

Manifolds and Brackets

The Slant Six's intake and exhaust manifolds can be removed together, as a set.

2 *This engine has a broken manifold mounting stud at the rear location. It also still has the original embossed steel shim type intake/ exhaust manifold gasket. Aftermarket Slant Six manifold gaskets are made from a composite material that seals better on previously used surfaces.*

1 *It is a good idea to spray some penetrating fluid onto the nut, washer, and stud assemblies before loosening the nuts. Use a long extension to reach the nuts in the middle of the manifolds. Do not worry about getting all the washers off the studs; they will drop off when you remove the manifolds.*

3 *The broken rear manifold mounting stud led to a burned and blown-out manifold gasket at the number-six exhaust port. Careful manifold installation using the correct fasteners and torque is required in order to prevent the Slant Six's exhaust manifold end studs from breaking.*

Water Pump, Damper, Sheet Metal, and Timing Chain

Stand the engine up on its end to remove the next group of parts. Lower the engine onto the ground and move the lift point to the front, then use the hoist to stand the engine onto its back end. This orientation makes it easy to remove the vibration damper, water pump, timing chain cover, timing chain, camshaft, oil pan, and cylinder head. It is a good idea to put cardboard and rags under the engine if you want to keep your floor clean.

1 *Lower the engine onto a hard surface and move the lift chain to the 3/8-16 UNC tapped hole in the front of the cylinder head, then use the hoist to lift and set the engine on its end. This orientation will make it easy to remove many of the parts.*

2 *Let the hoist do the work. With the lift chain attached to the alternator slider bracket mounting hole, lift the engine onto its end. Put a block of wood under the end of the cylinder head, making sure that the valve cover does not rest on it. The block will help stabilize and level the engine while it is on its end.*

Water Pump, Damper, Sheet Metal, and Timing Chain CONTINUED

3 You must use a bolt-on puller to remove the harmonic damper. Do not use a jaw-type puller that grips around the outer V-belt edge or you'll pull the V-belt ring off the center hub of the damper. You can rent, borrow, or make a bolt-on puller, so do not waste time trying other types. My homemade puller is a bar with a center hole and two outer holes that are spaced 1.6 inches from the center.

5 There are two sets of holes in the Slant Six damper hub. Three holes have 5/16-18 UNC threads, and the other three have 3/8-16 UNC threads. Watch for this difference when mounting the puller. Using an air impact wrench makes damper removal easy, but you can use a hand wrench if you keep the crankshaft from spinning while you tighten the puller's center bolt. I use a large adjustable wrench to hold the puller while I tighten the center drive bolt.

7 There are four oil pan bolts that screw into the bottom of the timing chain cover. These bolts are a little longer than the others, so keep track of them. I find it easier to remove the oil pan before taking off the timing chain cover. An old-fashioned speed wrench is nice to have if air tools are not available.

4 The front of every Slant Six crank-shaft is threaded, but the damper is press fitted onto the crankshaft. It usually did not come with a retaining bolt. Bolt-on harmonic damper pullers usually have a large swivel end on the drive bolt that can damage the threads in the front of the crankshaft. To prevent thread damage to the nose of the crankshaft, remove the puller's end or use a spacer in the threaded hole of the crankshaft.

6 With the damper off, remove the timing chain cover and water pump bolts. Bag and label the bolts or take a photo that shows the size of the bolts and where they go.

8 The back of the oil pan has two long bolts that screw into the alumi-num main seal retainer cap. Label or photo-graph them for future reference. With the oil pan removed, take note of the oil pickup tube's position relative to the floor of the oil pan. The pickup's fingerprint that was left behind in this oil pan shows that the pickup tube was on the floor of the oil pan and well centered.

9 The timing chain cover, water pump, oil pan, and valve covers can get baked on over the years, so you may need to give them a tap with a hammer to break them loose. If you need to give the cover a hard hit to loosen it, use a block of wood between the hammer and the cover.

10 Use a small pipe wrench or locking pliers to unscrew the oil pickup tube. Try to grip the tube at the widest point of a bend to prevent crushing or distorting it. The oil pickup tube matches the oil pan, so keep the tube with the oil pan it belongs with.

11 All Slant Six engines should have an oil slinger in front of the crankshaft's (lower) timing gear sprocket. Slide the cup-shaped slinger off the nose of the crankshaft and note how the cupped side faces outward. Save the slinger to be reused during engine reassembly.

12 This engine has a nylon top timing gear that shows wear and a lot of slop in the chain. These parts will need to be replaced. Pay special attention to the opening between the water pump pocket and the engine block's water jacket. The nail is pointing to an area known for casting flash and parting line mismatch that may need removal during engine block preparation.

13 Remove the timing gear to camshaft retaining bolt and washer, then pry the gear upward to free it from the camshaft. Keep track of the factory cam gear retaining bolt and washer because these are specially heat treated, and you will need them later.

14 Remove the oil pump retaining bolts and twist the pump to break it loose from the gasket. Slide the oil pump out of the engine block. The splash shield typically serves as the washers for the top two oil pump retaining bolts, but this engine had a washer on one of these bolts. You can also see the vehicle's VIN stamped into the rear of the lifter rail on this engine.

15 Oil pump to camshaft gear failure is a known problem with replacement Slant Six oil pumps. Carefully inspect the gear on the oil pump you remove. Save the factory gear for reuse if it has a smooth and well-centered contact pattern.

Valve Gear, Cylinder Head, and Camshaft

Remove the rocker arm assembly and all the pushrods as the first step toward removing the cylinder head. This gets the pushrods out of the way so they do not hang up on and/or bend as the heavy cylinder head is separated from the engine. Place all the special rocker arm shaft hold-down hardware in a labeled bag or container so it does not get lost or mixed up with other fasteners. Loop wire through the end holes of the rocker arm assembly's shaft to prevent the rocker arms and spacers from sliding off the shaft ends.

Be sure that at least one of the clamps holding the coolant bypass hose is loose so the hose pulls off cleanly as the head is removed. Do not cut or throw away the old bypass hose. It can be used as a length guide when cutting a new section of hose during engine reassembly.

The oil pump, fuel pump, dis-tributor, damper, timing chain cover, and gears must all be removed in order to get the camshaft out of the engine. Double-check to be sure that none of those parts are still attached. All of the lifters must be removed or pushed away from the camshaft lobes to make space for cam removal. The cam must be lifted straight out of its bore in order to prevent damage to the cam bearings.

1 *The rocker arms, pushrods, and cylinder head bolts are accessible once the valve cover is removed.*

2 *The valve spring pressure will want to push the rocker arm shaft upward as you loosen the retaining bolts, so start at the center of the shaft and only loosen the bolts one turn. Continue to break all the bolts loose, working outward toward both ends. Once loose, go back and continue to loosen them evenly so you do not bend the shaft as the bolts are removed. All of the pushrods will be released once the rocker arm assembly is off.*

3 *The pushrods will easily slide out of the lifter gallery once the rocker arm shaft is clear. On low-mileage engines, a lifter may stick to the end of the pushrod and come out with it. If this happens, bag and number the position if you want to reuse the cam, lifters, and pushrods. If you are doing a complete engine rebuild, there is no need to keep the lifters and pushrods in order because the lifters will need to be resurfaced or replaced when installing a new camshaft.*

4 *Be sure to loosen the coolant bypass hose clamps (or simply cut the hose) before trying to remove the cylinder head. The hose should already be off if the water pump has been removed. On engines with a distributor-side alternator mounting (most Slant Sixes), be sure the alternator's mounting bracket is removed so the head comes off easily without hanging up on the bracket.*

5 Remove the cylinder head bolts. An air impact gun makes an easy job out of removing these big, tight bolts, but you can also use a breaker bar to crack them loose and then use a speed wrench or your fingers to get the bolts all the way out. Be ready to "catch" a 75-pound cylinder head once the last head bolt is removed.

6 This engine still has the factory-embossed steel shim head gasket, so it is likely that it has never been disassembled. The head came right off once all the head bolts were out. Replacement composite head gaskets can stick to the surfaces, so you may need to lever the head off the block by putting a length of pipe or a crowbar into one of the head's ports and lifting the head.

7 I like to remove the camshaft when the engine is standing on its end. Install the top cam timing gear retaining bolt and washer, then give the cam a few rotations to push the lifters up and into their bores (away from the camshaft lobes). Keep the torque force on the bolt to a minimum because you will have to remove it immediately after rotating the cam.

8 Remove the timing gear to camshaft retaining bolt and move its large washer onto one of the cylinder head bolts. Thread the longer head bolt and washer assembly back into the camshaft and use it to grip and lift the camshaft out of the engine block. You may have to rotate and rock the camshaft side to side as you lift in order to clear all of the lifter ends and camshaft bearings.

Disassembly Inspection and Measurements

Mount the raw short-block onto an engine stand in order to visually inspect everything. It is also time to take cylinder bore and deck height measurements and complete the short-block disassembly work.

The most important disassembly measurement to take is the "as-is" deck height reading, which is the piston's top surface to the cylinder block's head gasket sealing surface. Deck height on a 170 (G) Slant Six is near or at zero when the engine is at top dead center (TDC), which means the top of the piston comes up even to the top of the bore in the block (deck). The factory deck height for a raised-block 225 or 198 (RG) Slant Six is a negative number, which means that the piston top does not reach the top of the cylinder bore at TDC.

At a minimum, take the deck height measurement at one cylinder and record that number. It is much better to take deck height readings at the number-1 and number-6 cylinders, to see if those measurements are the same. If you find a major height difference between the front and rear cylinder bores, take additional measurements at more locations.

The deck height dimension is essential information that is needed to calculate the engine's compression ratio. It is not uncommon to discover that the deck heights vary cylinder to cylinder on a Slant Six. That means that the compression ratio will be slightly different in each cylinder, leading to a rough-running engine. Seeing this issue now lets you pinpoint and correct the cause through additional measurements, machining, and/or part replacement.

Don't skip this measurement step, even if you plan to take the assembled short-block to the machine shop to complete the disassembly work. Knowledge about the engine you bring to the shop helps everyone, so spend the time to find out what you have, document your findings, and review them with the shop. The machine shop can confirm the issue and recommend the best way to correct the situation.

Disassembly and Measuring

1 With the head and sheet metal removed, the engine is easier to place on the engine stand. Lay the engine down and install the engine stand bracket onto it. Use one of the 7/16-14 UNC engine mount bracket-to-block bolts to attach a lift chain to one of the center head bolt holes.

2 Hoist the engine up and the engine stand will come up with it and swing into position. Lock the engine into an upright position so the lifters can be removed and you can take some deck height measurements.

3 The lifters are a uniform diameter, so they can be removed from the top or the bottom of the engine. I use a steel rod to push the lifters out through the bottom after the camshaft is removed and the engine is up on the engine stand. Pushing the lifters out through the bottom can prevent lifter bore damage that can be caused if the lifter face has been mushroomed or the lifter has a lot of carbon built up around its base.

4 Most of the parts removed from the engine should be sent to the machine shop for cleaning. Make a list of the items that you are leaving with the shop. The oil pump, water pump, and timing chain and gears will be replaced with new components, so you do not need to send those parts to the shop. Keep them around for reference (or as rebuild cores) while the engine is being rebuilt. If the camshaft is in good condition, you may want to send it to a camshaft shop for custom regrinding to your specifications.

5 Inspect the piston tops, cylinder bores, and ring ridges. Clear the carbon off the tops of the pistons with a wire brush or a one-edge razor blade and look for any stamped numbers or damage. This engine has smooth bore walls with little to no piston ring ridge at the top of each cylinder. Bores with long top-to-bottom scratches or two ring ridges will need to be rebored and honed to accept oversize pistons.

Disassembly and Measuring *CONTINUED*

7 The pistons in this engine are stamped 40, indicating that the bores and pistons are already 0.040 inch oversize. Confirm the number by measuring the actual bores and pistons, then use this information to decide if the engine can be rebuilt again and to order the correct size piston rings (.005, 0.010, 0.020, 0.030, 0.040, 0.060, or 0.080 inch). Oversize Slant Six pistons were offered over the years, but check piston and piston ring availability to be sure the size you need is actually available. Have the pistons and rings in your hands before boring an engine to any oversize dimension.

6 An inexpensive digital caliper is used to do an initial bore measurement across the top of the cylinders. Measurements on this engine confirmed that the cylinders are still at the standard 3.400-inch size, which makes it a good candidate for a simple rebuild. You will get a larger number if the piston tops are stamped with an oversize number. For example, a piston stamped .04 should have a cylinder that measures 3.440 inches.

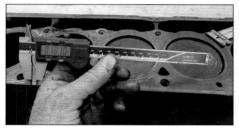

8 Use the depth probe end of a caliper to take the initial piston head to top deck surface measurements. This is an important measurement for compression ratio calculations, so take readings at the front and the back of each cylinder, along the piston pin centerline. These readings can indicate a warped or angle-machined deck surface. Write down the measurements. Your data can be used by the shop to correct any problems.

9 The Chrysler Slant Six deck height specifications are zero (0) for a 170 engine, -0.065 inch for a 198 engine, and -0.145 inch for a 225 engine. Zero and negative deck height measurements seem easy to take, but the actual readings can vary due to the piston rocking in the bore, uneven deck surface machining, uneven piston compression heights, bent connecting rods, or uneven connecting rod centers.

10 I use a special depth micrometer to help determine where and why the deck height is different around each cylinder bore. If you use a digital caliper and a stiff bar of material that spans across the cylinder, remember to subtract the bar's thickness from your readings.

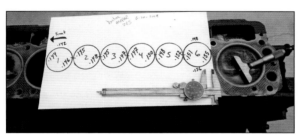

11 Draw a simple diagram and record piston to top deck measurements as you take them. The deck height on this engine increased as we moved front to back along the cylinder bores. This information can be used by the machine shop to verify and correct this issue during top deck resurfacing.

Pistons, Rods, Main Seal, and Crankshaft

The rotating assembly or "bottom end" of the engine contains the highest number of engine bearings. It is a common place to find problems. Crankshaft and connecting rod side clearance checks are simple and a good way to help determine if additional replacement parts or machine work will be needed. A failed crankshaft bearing will usually lead to additional machine work and/or expensive replacement parts.

You may want to consider finding a different engine to rebuild if you find a lot of spun bearings or damage to the crankshaft and connecting rods.

Visually inspect the rear main seal area to see if it shows any signs of oil leakage. If the outer main seal cap is oily, pay close attention to the main seal cap, the surrounding gaskets, and the seal itself. Identify any obvious reasons why it may be leaking and look for any evidence of

a history of oil leakage out the rear of the engine. Discovering the cause is critical to an effective repair of the main seal. Do not convince yourself that simply replacing the rear main seal itself will fix a rear oil leakage problem because most Slant Six engine rear main seal leaks are caused by part misalignment or improper assembly and not the seal itself.

1 Flip the engine over on the engine stand and inspect the crankshaft assembly. Look for signs of heat, such as burnt motor oil or metal discoloration. Wiggle each connecting rod cap. Side-to-side movement is normal, but there should not be any up-down movement in these bearings.

2 Use feeler gauges to check for connecting rod side clearance. The factory spec is 0.006 inch to 0.012 inch. Do not worry if the clearances are a little looser, but be concerned if the clearances are tight. Side clearances tighter than 0.006 inch reduce the oil flow through the bearing and may cause it to overheat and fail. A tight side clearance condition can easily be corrected by removing some material from either the connecting rod faces or the sides of the crankshaft journal, so now is the time to check.

3 Inspect the camshaft side of each main cap and connecting rod to be sure that they are clearly identified with a symbol or stamped number. Main caps have their position number cast into the cap. Number-1 is the front, number-4 is the rear, and number-3 is the thrust bearing. The connecting rod assembly's number does not need to match its actual position, but you will need markings to match each connecting rod with its cap. Confirm that there are sufficient marks to keep everything organized.

4 At first glance, it looked like the cap side stampings were missing on this engine's connecting rod assemblies. We cleaned the flat surfaces with a rag and carburetor cleaner to get a better look.

5 A closer look at the side of the connecting rods showed that the stamped number on the cap was not very deep, but it was still legible. There was a similar issue with the number-3 main cap number; it was distorted but still legible. We went ahead and removed all the connecting rod retaining nuts and main cap bolts.

6 The rear main seal retainer cap must be removed to get access to the heads of the number-4 main bearing cap bolts. I have seen three different types of bolt heads used to fasten the die-cast aluminum main seal retainer cap: Socket (Allen) head cap screws and 6- or 12-point 3/8-inch hex-head cap bolts with a washer face under the head. It is best to have a 12-point 3/8-inch socket on hand to remove either type of hex-head bolt. Keep track of these special fasteners; the small cap head makes them hard to replace if they get lost or damaged.

7 Make note of the oil pan's gasket seal around the rear main seal cap. The main seal cap has two L-shaped rubber inserts that seal the sides of the cap against the engine block. These L pieces extend out and onto the oil pan's sealing surface where the oil pan's side gaskets overlap them. This stack of gasket material is compressed by the oil pan to make a tight seal at the corner of the aluminum main seal cap.

8 You will need to carefully pry the real main seal cap out of the block's crankshaft pocket. Tilt the cap rearward to get it loose and then work it side to side with a screwdriver to get it all the way out of the block recess. Take a photo or mark the retainer so you know the direction of it for reinstallation. The bumps around the bolt heads face the crankshaft, so you can see the bolt heads when the oil pan is installed.

9 Here is a closer look at the main seal retainer and the L inserts that make the seal to the block. Bag, tag, and label the retainer. Be sure that the machine shop knows that it is an aluminum part because it cannot be cleaned in a caustic hot tank. Once cleaned, carefully inspect the cap for cracks and breakage around the pockets that hold the L seals.

10 The stack of gasket material at the corner of the aluminum main seal cap is shown here. The factory over-lapped the cork oil pan rail gaskets over the rubber L inserts that install into and extend out from under the main seal cap. This is a common leak point, so duplicate this gasket stacking during reassembly.

11 Position the crankshaft as shown so you have the best access to the outer connecting rod retaining nuts and caps. Remove all the nuts by using a 9/16 socket and then see how many of the rod caps you can get off by hand, by rocking them side to side. Don't worry if a bearing insert or two stick to the crankshaft journal.

Pistons, Rods, Main Seal, and Crankshaft CONTINUED

12 Use a screwdriver or pry bar to break loose any caps that do not come off easily by hand. Position the pry tool blade at the cap-to-rod parting line and pry on the joint as you wiggle the cap loose and off the bolts.

13 Rotate the crankshaft about 90 degrees to get better access to the center connecting rod caps. Remove these caps before unscrewing the main bearing cap bolts. Set aside all the connecting rod caps and nuts so they can be reunited with the connecting rods and pistons once they are removed from the engine block.

14 Try removing the main caps by rocking them front-to-back while gripping the two retaining bolts for some leverage. Three out of four should come off by using this technique. The number-3 main cap is the crankshaft's thrust bearing, so it will not allow front-to-back rocking; we will have to use a different approach to remove this cap.

15 Use a hammer to tap the sides of the number-3 main cap as you grip the retaining bolts and rock the cap around. The cap will work its way upward and free of the block as you tap its sides and wiggle the cap up. Small hammer taps are all you need to break the cap loose. Do not distort the block grooves that the cap fits into. These grooves and the cap's outer walls are the surfaces used to correctly register the main cap to the cylinder block. Don't damage them.

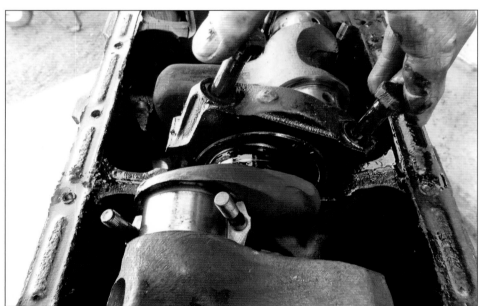

16 With the number-3 main cap off, we are ready to lift the crankshaft out of the engine. A Slant Six crankshaft weighs between 65 and 76 pounds, so it is a good idea to have some help when you remove it.

17 Grip the crankshaft at both ends and lift it straight up to clear all the bearings and connecting rods. Don't worry if some of the connecting rod bearings stick to the crankshaft or drop into the engine; you can collect them later. The goal is to get the crank out of the engine without dinging any of the bearing journal surfaces. I stand the crankshaft on end, but you can lay it down if you are concerned about knocking it over.

18 The connecting rod bearings are easy to remove by pushing them sideways. This motion breaks them free from the rod's machined surface and allows you to grip the bearing's edge and lift it out. We use the old bearing insert as connecting rod bore protection when pushing the piston and rod assemblies out because the inserts will be replaced with new ones.

19 Use the butt of a hammer handle or a soft piece of wood to drive each piston and connecting rod assembly out of the bores. Make sure the connecting rod is standing straight up so its big end does not hang up on the bottom edge of the cylinder bore as it drops out of the cylinder.

20 Place some old rags, carpet, or cardboard under the engine stand so you do not have to catch each assembly by hand as it drops out. Just about anything soft that can get greasy will work.

21 You can often push the piston and rod assembly up to the ring ridge by hand. The assemblies may drop out if there is no ring ridge at the top of the bores. If the assemblies stick, give each one a little tap. All of these pistons came out on the first tap and had a safe landing, as planned.

Pistons, Rods, Main Seal, and Crankshaft CONTINUED

22 Remove any old bearing inserts and reassemble the connecting rod cap to the matching connecting rod. Use the stamped numbers and the bearing tab notches as your guide. The stamped numbers, the bearing insert tab notches, and the rod's oil spurt hole are all on the same side of the connecting rod. Once the nuts are snug, the parting line should be smooth to the touch if everything is matched up and correctly assembled.

23 Inspect the position of the piston rings once the piston and rod assemblies are removed from the cylinders. We found that the ring gaps were aligned on one of the pistons. This can account for lower compression, increased oil consumption, and/or more carbon buildup in that cylinder.

Take Your Time!

It is important to take your time, take measurements, and document observations during engine disassembly. Diligence here will lead to a better outcome with your rebuilt Slant Six. A moment spent making sure rods and main caps are clearly numbered and documenting their proper installation orientation can save hours of head scratching and/or premature engine failure. Observing the position of the ring gaps as the pistons come out of the engine can help explain why an engine was using oil and help make the decision to simply re-ring the engine or to bore it oversize and buy new pistons. Knowing the actual bore size and deck heights gives you the information needed to calculate the actual compression ratios and decide on the exact amount of (and the way) material will be removed off the block and cylinder head surfaces.

We have quickly disassembled engines in the past, thinking that we are working fast and saving time, only to find that we have sent poor-quality or nonrepairable parts to the shop. We have also ended up spending additional time figuring out how things go back together, not knowing what we started with or understanding why the engine needed rebuilding in the first place. So we stress allowing time for careful disassembly and inspection. Take the measurements needed to do the math. Write the information down so you can pass it along to the shop accurately and refer back to it later.

BLOCK INSPECTION, PREPARATION, AND CLEANING

Slant Six engine blocks should be bare and ready for inspection and premachining preparation before they go out to the machine shop.

Once the engine is disassembled, visually inspect it for cracks. A rust stain is a sign of a nearby crack, so clean around any rust spot(s) and review that area closely under a bright light.

There are extra block preparation activities that should be done before delivering all the parts to the machine shop. Most of these tasks are optional but relatively easy, and they can make the difference between an average engine rebuild and a premium job. Do this work right after engine disassembly and initial crack inspection while the empty (and dirty) cylinder block is still on the engine stand.

These additional operations can be messy or leave behind metal chips.

Do the work now to avoid contaminating the cleaned block that has just come back from the machine shop.

Inspection

It is likely that you have spotted problems or areas of concern during disassembly. Now is the time to completely inspect the empty cylinder block and the head carefully. Make a list of any issues or areas of concern that you see so the machine shop can review those items and/or magnaflux the area(s). Here are the places to inspect carefully and what to look for:

Cracks in the Crankshaft Pocket

Look for the three long sand core parting lines in the crankshaft pocket of the block and inspect them for cracking. These parting lines run side to side between the base of the cylinder bores number-1 and number-2, number-3 and number-4, and number-5 and number-6. Raised or recessed parting lines form stress points where cracks usually start.

Damage in the Cylinder Bores

Cylinder bores must be smooth and round for the piston rings to seal.

Wipe down each bore with a rag and look for discoloration, damage, or rust that may indicate a crack or the need for sleeving. Cracks are usually found in the upper half of the bore, where the cylinder gets the hottest. Water sitting in a cylinder will cause rust pitting. A broken piston ring can scratch the cylinder wall to the point where the cylinder will need to be machined oversize. A piston pin that slips sideways and touches the bore or a broken piston and connecting rod can damage the cylinder wall to the point where a special sleeve will have to be installed in order to save the block.

Loose Main Caps or Galling

The main bearing caps need to fit tightly into recesses machined into the block, and the corresponding contact surfaces should be smooth so the main bearing inserts align correctly when the caps are installed. Caps that are loose in their saddles and/or have galled cap-to-block mating surfaces indicate that the engine was severely stressed, overheated, or was run after the main cap bolts lost torque. This type of damage is difficult to repair. It is best to use a different cylinder block that does not have this issue.

Main Bearing Bore Damage

Discoloration or spin marks in a main bearing bore indicate that the bearing insert has failed and spun in the bore. This condition can usually be corrected with special machine work called jig boring or main line honing (also called align-honing). If this is the case, it is usually better to find a different engine block. Not all machine shops have the special equipment needed to do main bearing bore remachining, and doing the work is expensive.

Loose or Discolored Camshaft Bearings

Camshaft bearings can also fail and spin in the bore they are pressed into. Check to see if the cam bearings' oil holes line up to the block's oil feed holes. Also check for any signs of discoloration or overheating around the cam bearings. In most cases, this condition can be fixed when new bearings are installed.

Damage in the Crank Pocket

Large dings, gouges, or scrape marks in the crankshaft pocket are usually caused by a past connecting rod failure or some other part getting caught in the spinning crankshaft. Minor damage is cosmetic and will never be seen once the engine is assembled. More severe damage should be inspected for cracks around the damaged area. The extreme example of this problem is an obvious hole punched through the side of the block, which was caused by a connecting rod breaking and getting hit by the spinning crankshaft.

Rust Stains and Drip Marks

Drip marks and/or rust stains on the outer block surfaces may indicate a crack. The most common place to find this condition is under the freeze plugs and along the head gasket seam. Do not simply think that these stains or rust marks are from a leaking freeze plug or from a blown head gasket. Be sure to clean off and inspect the areas carefully for cracks.

Damaged Threaded Holes

Stripped bolt holes are not uncommon and they can be repaired, but you want to know about all of the damaged fastener holes and have a repair plan before you move forward with rebuilding the engine. Low ten-

sion bolt holes that hold pans, covers, and brackets can be repaired with a Heli-Coil or rethreaded to the next larger size. The main cap, cylinder heads, and other large fasteners that require high torque loads are harder to repair. If you find problems with any of those threaded holes, consider replacing the block.

Casting Flaws

Sand casting flaws such as core shift, sintered sand, voids, dings, pits, and overgrinding of parting lines are common and should be reviewed carefully. You will have to decide if what you see is just ugly (in a place that no one will ever see), requires additional machining, or makes the part unusable. Welding and crack "pinning" is another flaw that shows up, and the repair should be evaluated for effectiveness.

Try to find the problems described above yourself and decide if you really want to move forward with the engine block or part before spending

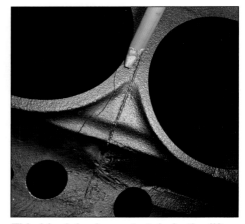

This block had a rust stain in the lifter bore area that was caused by large cracks at the base of the number-5 cylinder. A block with large cracks is not worth repairing, so this one was scrapped. Also note the hammer dings from the foundry workers knocking off casting flash.

time loading and delivering a nonserviceable item to the machine shop.

Cylinder Head to Engine Block Alignment

Clean off any pieces of old head gasket material or carbon with a wide putty knife. Place the cylinder head back onto the empty engine block. Hold the parts together snugly with a few head bolts. Then, flip the assembly over so you can inspect the head chambers through the empty crankcase and cylinder bores.

You want to see if the combustion chambers are well centered over the cylinder bores, so look closely for any combustion chamber edges that extend into the bore. Look for a consistent shift that can be corrected by repositioning the dowel pins.

The best case is to find chambers that are all well centered over the cylinder bores with a possible thin chamber edge or two and overhanging into random cylinder bores. Once you have the head centered as

This head to cylinder block check shows a misalignment that exposes a chamber edge along the spark plug side of the chambers on the forward cylinders. We pulled the front dowel pin and rechecked them while moving the head around on the block.

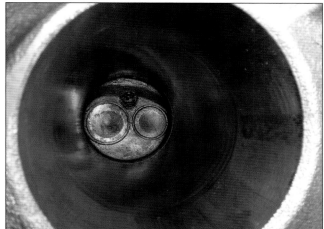

A well-centered cylinder head will not have chamber edges extending into the bore area. Sharp, thin edges of metal can superheat and cause preignition. Grind any remaining edges away once you have centered the head over all the bores.

Install the head onto the empty cylinder block to check the head's chamber alignment to the bores in the cylinder block. Bolt a used rocker arm shaft to the head to make a convenient lifting handlebar. This makes it easier to lift the head onto and off of the block while doing the checking and any adjustments.

best as possible, mark any remaining exposed edges with a long, sharp probe, remove the head, and grind those edges away to prevent a hot spot in the cylinder. Recheck and repeat as needed.

It is nice to do this work now so any grinding particles are cleaned away at the machine shop. This is "at risk" work. Do not put a lot of time into the cylinder head yet because the head will need to be disassembled, cleaned, and inspected to make sure it is crack free and suitable for a rebuild.

You may find a mismatch between the cylinder head's locating holes and the dowel pins that are pressed into the block's deck. This condition will show itself as an exposed chamber

edge in the same place in each cylinder bore. This means that the head is not well centered on the block. If you see this condition, it is best to pull out one or both of the dowel pins, reinstall the head, and recheck things.

Leave the retaining bolts a little loose so you can move the head around on the block. This will allow you to see if there is a place where all the chambers are well centered over the cylinders. If you find a good position, use offset (eccentric) dowel pins, turn or grind the tops of the pins undersize, or leave the pins out altogether and rely on added index marks between the head and block to find correct head-to-block alignment during final engine assembly.

The pins can also be removed by gripping and twisting them with a strong locking pliers. Use a screwdriver to pry upward as you rotate until the pin comes out. I have a special tool that removes dowel pins without damaging them. Purchase replacement 1/4x5/8-inch long dowel pins from McMaster-Carr, MSC Industrial Supply, Berg, etc. You can also file the plier marks smooth and reuse the old ones.

The dowel pins used to locate the cylinder head to the block are 1/4-inch diameter. They can be purchased with an eccentric offset if the combustion chamber to cylinder bore location needs to be adjusted. You can also braze and grind to make custom offsets, if needed.

Cylinder Head to Block Locating

1 The engine ID stamping pad on the top passenger-side corner of the block is a good place to grind or punch a cylinder head locating line or mark. Add these marks once you have the head well centered over the cylinder bores.

2 Cylinder head location marks at three of the four corners of the top deck are enough to correctly locate the head onto the block during final engine assembly. A ground flat combined with a punch mark is used here to indicate proper head location.

3 Ground flats across the block and head combined with punched or engraved marks give you two axis index markings, all in one place. Look for areas near the corners of the engine where the edges of the head and block are close to each other, and add your marks there.

Random alignment issues are usually caused by casting problems or extreme warping from overheating. The head and block are both suspect if the bore and chamber misalignment is inconsistent and severe. Testing a different head on the block (or vice versa) is the fastest way to confirm the problem. However, finding the true cause or correcting this type of issue may not be practical. Many times it is better to simply use a different part that does not have a major misalignment issue.

Deburring and Preparation

The following engine block modifications should be done to every Slant Six engine before sending it to the machine shop. This work is mostly focused on cooling and oiling system improvements that help the fluids flow to critical places and reduce parasitic drag.

The coolant entry point into the cylinder block's main water jacket is an area of concern because it needs to be smooth and as large as possible to ensure proper engine cooling. The transition point where the oil flows from the oil pump into the engine block's main oil passageways is another area where improvements can be made. Opening these passageways ensures proper oil flow to all the bearings and reduces the load on the delicate oil pump drive gears. Adding a large chamfer to the tops of the lifter bores and honing them out allows more oil to flow by the lifters and onto the critical lifter face to cam lobe surface. Adding extra oil drain holes in key places redirects oil to places where it is the most useful in terms of cooling and wear protection.

Water Pump Mounting Flange Smoothing

1 *There are casting parting lines and raised casting flash between the water pump's mounting flange pocket and the entrance to the block's water jacket. Obstructions in this area reduce coolant flow and create turbulence. Grind away excess metal and increase the size of this opening to avoid issues.*

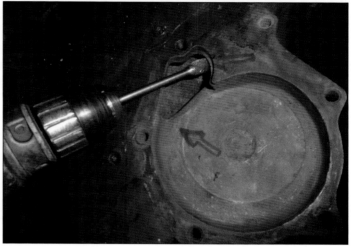

2 *The water pump rotates clockwise, so focus your grinding work on increasing size at the bottom of the opening and removing the sharp inside edge along the top of the opening. Break all the edges and smooth out surrounding surfaces to reduce water flow turbulence.*

3 *Run your finger along all of the inner edges of the opening and "think like water." Grind smooth any bumps or sharp corners. Try to open up the water jacket entry point to help improve the coolant flow. Use a small grinding tool to get into the tight corners.*

4 *A smooth transition around the corners will reduce the amount of energy needed to move the coolant from the water pump and into the engine block. Do a little polishing at the entrance to create the smooth transition.*

Taps and Passageway Preparation

1 *Most Slant Six engine blocks have a thick boss at the rear of the main oil gallery. Some engine blocks come from the factory with this boss already drilled and tapped for 1/8-inch dry-seal (NPT) pipe thread. Not this block, so we drilled and tapped the boss during the rebuild.*

2 *The NPT tap has a tapered thread. Be sure to use the recommended 11/32 drill size and put a chamfer at the top of the hole to help get the tap started.*

3 *Some of the oil system modifications put metal chips into the main oil gallery. Remove the front and rear gallery plugs to be sure that this important passageway gets absolutely clean at the machine shop.*

4 *The rear oil gallery plug is next to the camshaft expansion plug. It can be more difficult to access when the block is on the engine stand. Use a wrench in combination with the correct driver to get access and leverage. Heat the plug if it does not want to crack loose.*

5 *Grind smooth the sharp corners where the oil flows from the oil pump into the two branches of the block's main oil gallery. My preferred tool is a 5/8-inch (0.625-inch) ball burr on a long shank, but any grinding burr or stone between 1/2-inch and 5/8-inch diameter will do the job. Run the tool backward to get the cut started because it will want to jump around or jam at first.*

6 Grind as smooth a radius onto the edges of the hole's entry point as possible. Doing this helps oil flow and reduces turbulence. This photo shows the grinding work we did on the entry to the front branch of the oil gallery.

7 Repeat the process on the rear oil gallery entrance hole. Open up the hole's entrance and round off the sharp edges as much as you can. Unrestricted oil flow at this intersection reduces the energy needed to turn the oil pump and decreases the load on the oil pump's drive gear.

8 A common wear spot in a Slant Six is a groove worn into the fuel pump eccentric on the camshaft. The eccentric's surface relies on oil splash and mist for lubrication. Dirty or old motor oil combined with low engine speeds can starve this area of needed lubrication. I drill an extra oil return hole above the eccentric to direct more oil onto it.

9 Work from the crankcase side to find the clearance recess for the fuel pump actuation arm. Start a hole as close to the cylinders as possible by drilling straight down. The new hole needs to exit on the cylinder bore side above the cam in order for the collected oil to drop onto the eccentric when the engine is slanted 30 degrees.

10 Complete the hole by drilling at an angle until it breaks through near the outer wall of the lifter and pushrod pocket above. The 30-degree slant of the engine will have rocker arm assembly oil collecting along this wall, so we want that return oil to go down our new hole.

Taps and Passageway Preparation *CONTINUED*

11 Turn the engine over and deburr the top of the new hole by adding a large countersink or radius. The goal is to create a funnel that will direct as much oil as possible down this feed hole.

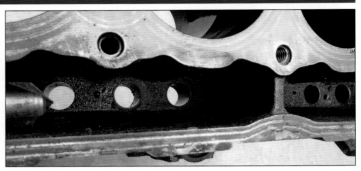

12 Inspect the top of each lifter bore and countersink the top edge, especially if it has a sharp corner. The lifter bores are 0.904 diameter, so a 1-inch cutter works well. The lifter pocket is 4 inches deep, so the tool needs an extended shank to get to the top of each bore. The tool I use has an 8-inch shank length.

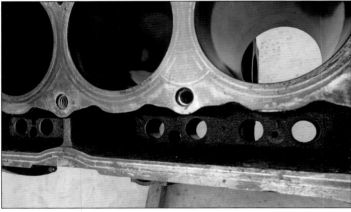

13 A large 45-degree cut will aid in lifter installation and also holds some oil around the lifter. Use a small brake cylinder hone or a rolled-up piece of sandpaper to deburr the edge of the new countersink and smooth out the lifter bores.

14 It is easier to work from the crankcase side when honing or sanding the lifter bores. Limit the depth of the hone strokes so the tool does not drop out the other side of the bore while you hone. Use an old lifter to check your work by installing it from the top. If everything is properly deburred and smooth, it should start into the lifter bore easily and drop right through.

There is a 1/4-18 NPT water jacket drain plug on the passenger's side of the block near the rear. Remove this plug and poke through the sediment that you may find. Doing this will help the final water jacket cleaning and rinsing process. Save and reuse the plug or buy a new one if it is badly corroded or damaged.

Remove the block's expansion plugs (freeze plugs) by first knocking them into the water jacket with a steel rod or socket. Twist them sideways once they are loose and pull them out through their hole with pliers.

Cleaning

There are a few different ways the machine shop cleans engine parts. The common processes are jet wash (hot water washing), baking (hot oven), and hot tank (hot caustic soda solution). Discuss with your machine shop which method they will use and the costs associated with them.

To prepare your block for machine shop cleaning, remove the freeze plugs and drain plugs. Poke around in the water jackets with a long screwdriver or ice pick to loosen rust scale and remove any leftover sand casting core wires. These wires are commonly found in the cylinder head, and they can be pulled out with needle-nose pliers. Time spent mechanically removing rust and sludge from the water jackets helps get them clean when the block is hot tanked or power washed. You can get the water jackets in the engine block and cylinder head completely clean by etching them out with strong acid prior to sending the parts to the machine shop.

Now that disassembly, inspection, and premachining of the cylinder block and the head preparation is complete, it is time to deliver the engine and parts to the machine shop for any needed precision machine work. Only send the items that need cleaning and machining, and make a list of what you leave at the shop. The goal is to get the engine back from the shop in a "ready to assemble" condition so you can immediately build it once you get everything back.

Supercleaning the Water Jackets

1 Install temporary rubber freeze plugs if you are going to acid etch the water jacket area. Use Dorman part number 10232 or search the Internet using "1-5/8, rubber, freeze, expansion, test, plug" word combinations as key search terms.

2 If you are etching just the engine block water jackets, use a noncorrosive (plastic) water pump block-off plate and plug all openings, including the timing chain cover through hole. Install the cylinder head onto the block and stand the assembly on end if you want to etch the block and head at the same time. You will need an easy way to drain the dirty acid once the etching is finished.

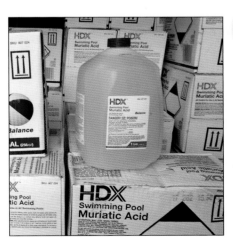

3 Muriatic acid works well for removing rust scale, and it is available at most hardware and pool supply stores. If you are going to use acid for cleaning, remember to use all recommended safety gear and handle any acid carefully.

4 Level out the engine block in a place where spilled acid will not stain or corrode surrounding surfaces. Pour the acid into the water jackets and let it work for a few days. Drain the used acid back into its original containers, then flush the block and surrounding area with water and baking soda to neutralize any remaining acid.

Machine Shop Selection and Activities

Most people do not overhaul a lot engines, so they are not familiar with the specialized automotive machine shops that do all of the precision machining work needed for a successful engine rebuild. As with most specialty jobs, it is best to get automotive machine shop recommendations from others who have already done major engine repair work and then make some phone calls to get price quotes.

You can quickly get an idea of shop costs by requesting a quote for a "complete rebuild" on a Chrysler Slant Six, including assembly labor. Most people reading this book want to do the engine assembly themselves, and if that is the case for you, prepare a list of the machining work you want done and parts you will be suppling to the shop. Use the list as the basis for a discussion with the shops you felt good about when you initially called.

You need to have a comfort level with the people doing the work to your parts. The first step to be comfortable with a shop is to ask if it has ever rebuilt a Chrysler Slant Six engine or other inline 6-cylinder engines. You want to see if the shop is knowledgeable and interested in your project and if it is listening to your desires. The next step is to see if you can have a constructive two-way conversation about your needs and wants for the engine. Try to determine if the shop has "an engine is an engine" attitude.

There are some activities that machine shops commonly do to rebuild an engine. We split the activities up into *always*, *often*, and *sometimes* categories based on the engine's initial condition, your skill level, and your budget.

Always: This is work we have the shop do, even if the engine we started with was in perfect condition when we took it apart (just needs new "rings and bearings").

Often: This is the always work plus additional machining that is required on a well-worn engine to make it like new.

Sometimes: This is work you can do yourself or is nice to have, such as rebalancing the rotating assembly or porting the cylinder head.

Here are the items that I put in each category:

Always
- Clean the engine block, head, internal parts, and sheet metal
- Resurface ("deck") the block and cylinder head for flatness and added compression
- Inspect the connecting rods (big-end to specifications)

Often
- Install new camshaft bearings into the block
- Bore the engine block to the new piston size (must have the new pistons to measure)
- Recondition the connecting rods
- Install new pistons onto the connecting rods
- Regrind the crankshaft (FYI, most shops send crankshafts out to be ground by a specialist)
- Install new valve guides or valve seats into the head

Sometimes
- Port and rebuild the cylinder head (I prefer to port and assemble my cylinder head; however, if you don't have the skill level this may be a good job for the machine shop)
- Rebalancing the engine
- Assembly work on the short- or long-block

The list does not include work needed for the camshaft, lifters, and oil pump. In the past, these were reground or rebuilt, but they are simply replaced these days. The list of machine work requiring special equipment is relatively short, so most of the engine rebuilding cost is for replacement parts and the assembly labor time. ■

A jet wash machine is like a big dishwasher for engine parts. The machine has a rotary table inside and uses soap and hot water to do the cleaning. This type of equipment has replaced many of the hot tanks that used to be found in automotive machine shops.

Crankshaft grinding is a high-precision activity that is done on an expensive machine. Smaller machine shops usually send crankshafts out to be ground by a specialty shop. You can have the crank grinder provide the matching undersize bearing (a crankshaft kit) or purchase the bearings yourself. (Photo Courtesy Steve Magnante)

Select a machine shop that has resurfacing equipment that uses cutting inserts instead of a grinding stone. The cutting insert machine can take off more material per pass, which is better for a Slant Six engine. The Slant Six usually requires a heavy cut on the cylinder block and/or head to boost compression.

Bore the cylinder block and install oversize pistons if the wear and top-to-bottom taper exceeds 0.008 inch. Round, straight, and rigid cylinders promote good ring sealing, so do not bore out the cylinders more than what is needed to get a clean, straight bore.

The early Slant Six head has a combustion chamber that is slightly smaller on the spark plug side. The chamber on these heads will begin to close as the head is machined for higher compression. (Photo Courtesy Steve Magnante)

The cylinder bores must be measured for wear plus a cleanup allowance. This allowance is added so you can order the correct oversize piston. You should have the replacement pistons prior to finish cylinder honing. This allows the shop to measure the pistons for proper cylinder bore clearance and fit.

The connecting rod resizing equipment has a special inspection gauge used to measure the size and the roundness of the rod's bores. Have the shop measure your rods and recondition them if any are out of specifications. Many of the Slant Six connecting rods we measure are well within specifications and can be reused with a simple cleanup.

SHORT-BLOCK ASSEMBLY

Once you have everything back from the machine shop, you've reached the point where the focus shifts to assembling all the parts that were carefully disassembled, cleaned, inspected, and machined. Correct assembly is critical to engine performance and longevity, so be sure to have the right parts, tools, knowledge, and working conditions to do a proper assembly job.

Allow yourself enough time to do any particular step; avoid rushing through an operation or stopping and starting during an important process. It is best to have everything together before starting the engine assembly work. Make a list to be sure you have the items you need, when you need them.

Assembly Area and Operations

A clean and well-lit area for engine assembly is important, so do some housekeeping before starting work. Make sure all floors and workspaces are clear of dirt and debris. Clear workbench space so you can spread out parts as you begin each assembly.

Engine Rebuild Checklist

Here is a sample checklist you can use as a starting point for your list:

Machine Shop
- ❑ Engine block (cleaned and machined)
- ❑ Camshaft bearings (installed)
- ❑ Crankshaft and bearings (correct size and type)
- ❑ Piston and connecting rods (cleaned, machined, and assembled)
- ❑ Cylinder head (cleaned, machined, and assembled)
- ❑ Sheet metal, fasteners, and oil pickup tube (cleaned)
- ❑ Manifolds (resurfaced or replaced)
- ❑ Radiator (serviced or replaced)

Purchased Parts
- ❑ Piston rings
- ❑ Camshaft and lifters

- ❑ Timing set and oil slinger
- ❑ Oil, water, and fuel pumps (if needed)
- ❑ Freeze plugs
- ❑ Gasket set and sealers (RTV, pipe dope, and adhesive)
- ❑ Spark plugs and wires (if needed)
- ❑ Thermostat (if needed)

Supplies
- ❑ Grease and lubricants (assembly lube, moly grease, anti-seize and spray lube)
- ❑ Plastigauge: in sizes green (0.001 to 0.003) and red (0.002 to 0.006)
- ❑ Spray paint
- ❑ Hoses and belts (if needed)
- ❑ Oil, air, and fuel filters
- ❑ Antifreeze and coolant
- ❑ Engine oil
- ❑ Cam break-in additive (optional) ∎

The sequence of operations we provide in this chapter allows the best access to subassemblies and for the parts you are installing. For example, you need to torque the main cap bolts before installing the rear main seal cap because the main seal cap blocks access to the number-4 main cap bolt heads.

Painting

It is best to paint the engine block and cylinder head as soon as they come back from the machine shop. This is the time when the parts should be completely clean. Wipe off any fingerprints or oil stains and give the outer bare metal surfaces a good coat of paint. Doing the first coat of paint now helps with paint adhesion and makes future cleanups and drying easier.

Special engine paint is not really needed unless you are matching the exact Chrysler engine paint type and color for a factory original restoration project. There are many choices for paint brands and paint colors, so refer to the engine identification section for information on Slant Six engine colors used throughout the years. High-temperature paint is not needed except for exhaust manifolds, pipes, or components (the factory did not paint these items). In the end, decisions on paint color and the quality of the engine's overall paint job are up to the owner of the vehicle. Do what you want and don't waste a lot of time and money on it.

Painting the Block

This partially painted Slant Six engine block highlights the areas that are easily seen once the engine is assembled and installed in the vehicle. Be sure to get an especially nice coat of paint onto the surfaces shown.

3 The main oil gallery area should be painted on the passenger's side of the engine. Remember that the engine will be slanted 30 degrees to the passenger's side so there will not be much showing on this side of the engine.

1 The engine block, cylinder head, and any other parts should be completely clean when you get them back from the machine shop. Wipe them down and give them a coat of paint to prevent rust and to make future cleanups easier.

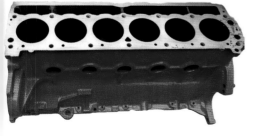

2 The first coat of paint on the driver's side of the engine block focuses on the front area, especially the back of the water pump's mounting flange. The lower pan rail and starter motor socket are also visible once the engine is assembled and installed. The unpainted area shown is under the manifolds, so it only needs a light coat of paint.

4 Keep paint off the head gasket's sealing area. You can wipe off any overspray that gets onto that surface. The final paint job results on the driver's side are shown here.

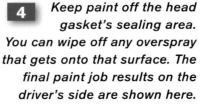

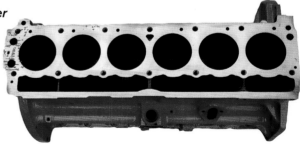

5 This view gives you a good idea of what will be seen on the passenger's side of the engine. Cover everything with paint, but do not waste paint or spend a lot of time painting areas that will never be seen.

Once painting is done, do a final review of the engine block to check the thread quality and countersink depths at the entry of all the threaded bolt holes. The head bolt hole chamfers may be small or missing if you had the block's top deck machined for additional compression. Spend time running a tap through each of the threaded holes. Remove any sharp edges and deburr everything that can cut or scratch you as you do the assembly job.

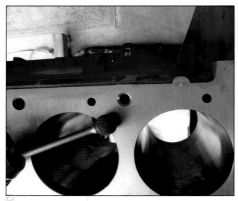

Check the countersink depth and symmetry on all the threaded holes and chamfer any countersinks that are light or missing. This is especially important on the threaded head bolt holes if the top deck was resurfaced for increased compression.

Run a tap through each of the threaded holes to clean out debris and ensure that the fastener starts easily. Be sure to do this work before final cleaning so any metal chips can be washed out afterward.

Wash Out Remaining Debris

The final preparation activity before engine reassembly is washing all parts with soap and water. Use a toilet bowl brush and bottle brushes

Deburr or grind smooth any sharp edges or ugly casting flaws you saw during the final inspection of the bare engine block. Look for any edge or protrusion that may cut or scratch you as you assemble the engine and round off or break those edges.

Give the bare engine block a good soap and water wash before starting the assembly process. Having a selection of brushes is key to getting into all the tight spots and passageways. The main oil gallery and cross-holes to the main bearings must be completely clean prior to installing the passageway plugs.

to get into the cylinders and all the oil passages. Use plenty of hot water. Once clean, blow the engine dry and coat any freshly machined surfaces with a light oil or spray lubricant, to prevent rust.

Direct a stream of water into each side of the main oil galleries and occasionally plug the holes to force the water through the passages leading to the main bearings. Be sure to brush clean and thoroughly flush out the threaded camshaft side main cap bolt holes. These holes break into the oil feed cross-holes to the main bearings, and any dirt left in these threads will be pushed down and into the oiling system when the bolts are installed.

The main oil gallery to main bearing cross-holes also deliver oil to the camshaft bearings. Make sure those holes are clean and that water flows out of all the camshaft bearings. If you do not see water flowing out onto any of the cam bearing surfaces, check the cam bearing installation for proper oil hole alignment.

Tools Needed to Assemble a Slant Six

- Socket set (3/8- and 1/2-inch drive preferred)
- 12-point 3/8 socket (likely needed for the rear main seal cap bolts)
- Combination wrench set
- 5/16 (0.312) Allen wrench (oil galley plugs)
- Assorted pliers and screwdrivers
- Files and sandpaper
- Torque wrench (up to 100 ft-lbs)
- Piston ring compressor
- Feeler gauges
- Degree wheel (metal or printed on paper)

- 6-inch dial caliper
- Putty knife and razor blades
- Hammer
- Engine assembly lubricant (thicker grease is preferred for bearing surfaces)
- High-pressure molybdenum disulfide grease (for threads, cam lobes, and gear surfaces)
- Straight 30-weight engine oil (for piston rings, cylinders, and timing chain)
- Anti-seize grease (for manifold and exhaust system fasteners) ∎

Reassemble the Slant Six

The first reassembly step is to install the oil gallery plugs and rear camshaft plug (if needed). Use pipe thread sealer on any threaded plugs and a sticky sealer, such as Tack Seal or weatherstrip adhesive, on any expansion plugs (freeze plugs).

Be sure to use the proper low-profile socket head plugs at the ends of the main oil gallery. These short NPT plugs are needed in order to clear the timing chain's top gear in front and the flex plate at the rear of the engine.

Be sure that the rear cam plug and the main oil gallery plugs (front and rear) are installed in the block. Use a small amount of sealer to prevent leaks. Our shop did not install these important plugs, so we did.

Camshaft Installation

The camshaft in a Slant Six has a gear in the center that directly drives the distributor and oil pump. These gears can wear out prematurely and fail, causing loss of oil pressure and contaminating the engine with metal filings. This is a known trouble spot with the Slant Six, so it is important to carefully inspect and prepare the camshaft and its gear before installation.

Check the cam gear to oil pump gear tooth contact pattern to make sure the gears are meshing correctly and have smooth tooth contact surfaces. For the best access and visibility, do the cam to oil pump gear mesh inspection work early in the assembly process before installing the crankshaft and piston assemblies.

Pro Mechanic Tech Tip

We use a Slant Six cylinder head bolt as a handle when installing the cam. This way, we don't ding or scratch the new camshaft bearings during camshaft installation. ∎

The front oil gallery plug is a low-profile pipe plug. It must be installed for the engine to get oil pressure.

Prepping and Installing the Camshaft

1 Sudden loss of oil pressure during new engine break-in is usually caused by camshaft to oil pump drive gear failure. Soft gear material used on replacement oil pumps, rough tooth surfaces, or misaligned gear contact loads can all lead to early oil pump gear failure. It is a good idea to reuse the gear off your used factory oil pump if it shows little to no wear.

2 The edges of the camshaft gear can be sharp and ragged, so carefully break those edges with a small file or a grinding wheel. If a cam walks forward in the block and the contact pattern moves off the edge, a smooth, rounded cam gear edge will not damage the mating gear tooth. The rounded edges will also let more oil onto the gear faces.

3 There are two important oil holes in the rear camshaft journal. The first is the large front-to-back hole (blue wire) that prevents oil pressure from building up between the end of the cam and the expansion plug. Oil pressure here will push the cam forward and/or pop the expansion plug out of the block. The second hole is the small cross-hole through the rear journal (thin wire) that allows pressurized oil into a passageway to the rocker arm assembly. This cross-hole needs to line up to the feed holes in the rear cam bearing. Make sure the cross-hole is not misdrilled or plugged.

4 Check the cross-hole in the rear cam journal with a loose cam bearing. All of the holes should align once per revolution of the camshaft. This cam's cross-hole was slightly misdrilled, so it was lengthened with a small grinding wheel. You can also center punch and drill right next to the existing hole in order to create the oil pathway.

5 Install the camshaft and make sure it turns freely in the cam bearings. To make rotating the cam easy, screw a top timing gear with a knob onto the camshaft or use a socket and a speed wrench to rotate the cam.

6 Gear checking paste or grease can be used to inspect the gear mesh. Instead, we use fine lapping compound so we can smooth the gear faces along with doing the contact pattern check. Apply the lapping compound to both gears and install the oil pump.

7 Use a couple of bolts to hold the oil pump in place while you rotate the camshaft from the front of the engine.

8 Turn the camshaft clockwise as fast as possible. Place your finger onto the oil pump gear to apply a little drag and to help push the lapping compound back into the tooth contact area.

9 You will feel and hear the polishing action and see the lapping compound spread out and cover all the teeth. A visible contact pattern will start to develop. Add more lapping compound if more polishing is needed.

10 The contact pattern on this oil pump gear is uniform and well centered. The matching pattern on the camshaft gear is acceptable but slightly off-center, toward the rear. To better center the contact mark on the cam's gear, add a shim between the camshaft (top) timing gear and the front cam face. Adding a shim will move the entire camshaft rearward and shift the gear's contact point.

11 Once the gear check and polishing work is finished, use a good solvent to wash all the lapping compound off the gears. Use a stiff brush to get between all the gear teeth and rinse thoroughly. You do not want lapping compound to get into your motor oil!

12 Apply lubricant to the cleaned camshaft prior to installation. Apply molybdenum disulfide paste on the cam lobes and the gear but not the journals. Use standard engine assembly lube or motor oil on the cam bearings and journals.

13 With good access to the lifter bores from the crankcase area, apply a light coat of engine assembly lube to each bore. Use your finger and feel each lifter bore as you lubricate it, to make sure it is smooth and clean.

14 Guide the cam lobes and gear through the cam bearings using a cylinder head bolt in the front of the camshaft and your other hand at the rear. Rotate the cam once it is installed to make sure it spins freely.

Crankshaft Bearing Identification

Crankshaft installation includes the main bearings and rear main seal. There are three types of Slant Six main bearings and two styles of rear main seals, so review the replacement parts to be sure the main bearings have the correct oil feed holes and the main seal style will successfully seal the engine.

Main bearings for the forged crankshaft are 1.032 inches wide or 1 1/32 inches. The bearings used in the 1976 and later cast-crank engine are 0.873 inch wide (7/8 inch). Forged-crankshaft main bearings used in cast-iron engine blocks only. Have one oil feed hole in the grooved upper insert. Main bearings used in the cast-iron and the aluminum-block Slant Six have two oil feed holes.

Most aftermarket replacement main bearing inserts for the forged-crank Slant Six come with two oil feed holes. It is a good policy to always check, especially if you are building an aluminum-block engine. The factory used a special upper grooved main bearing insert with a chamfered edge in the number-1 location to send pressurized oil out to the timing chain. Check your replacement main bearing inserts for this feature.

Main Seal

The factory installed asbestos-graphite rope seals in most Slant Six gaskets. The rope seal is more forgiving and seals better against the knurled (serrated) seal surface found on most Slant Six crankshafts. Today's aftermarket gasket sets include a two-piece neoprene synthetic rubber lip seal. There are a number of misalignment problems that can occur with the two-piece lip seal, so mock it up in the empty block and inspect it before installing the crankshaft.

To check the alignment, make sure the two molded rubber seal insert sections align with each other. Also check the assembly's alignment to the crankshaft's centerline. Use an arbor or straightedge to be sure you get complete lip contact and compression.

A leaking main seal is a difficult repair to make after assembly is complete, so take the time to check the seal's fit. Be sure to assemble the seal sections correctly. When in doubt, use a rope seal, especially if you see misalignment, uneven lip compression, or a rough sealing surface on the crankshaft.

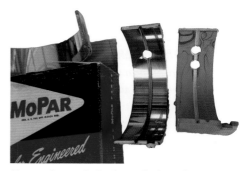

Forged-crankshaft Slant Six main bearings are wider than the 1976 and later cast-crankshaft bearings. Getting incorrect late main bearings is a common problem when building the earlier forged-crank engines. Check the main bearings you have prior to starting the assembly work.

Forged crankshaft main bearings were made with one or two oil feed holes. Either type works in a cast-iron block, but the two-hole bearing is required when building an aluminum-block Slant Six. The good news is that all of today's aftermarket main bearings for the forged-crank Slant Six are the two-hole type.

These original old stock Chrysler main bearings have one oil feed hole. They can only be used in a cast-iron block. The grooved number-1 main bearing insert has a large 45-degree edge break (chamfer) that allows oil to spray out onto the timing chain and oil slinger. To improve timing chain lubrication, file a larger edge break onto the upper number-1 insert on aftermarket replacement main bearings.

Sealing the Main Seal

1 Slant Six rear main seals come in two types: the rope seal and the lip seal. The lip seal is easier to install, but it will leak if there is misalignment between the seal and the crankshaft centerline or if the mating knurled surface on the crank is rough. Inspect the lip seal's contact integrity before deciding which type of main seal to use.

2 The two sections of this lip seal do not align well when installed. This can often be corrected by changing to a different seal retainer, such as the aluminum main seal cap.

3 A straightedge can be used to see if a lip-type main seal is well centered on the crankshaft. Be sure the taper of the lip seal faces to the outside of the engine. Offset the ends of the seal inserts so they do not line up with the joints between the main seal cap and block.

4 Get a more accurate lip seal compression and centering check by using an arbor. This tool registers off the main bearing inserts and extends out to the seal's lip. Use a 2.750-inch-diameter pipe that is at least 10 inches long. The actual main seal surface on the crankshaft is larger (2.812-inch diameter) so there should be a slight gap all the way around the seal's lip when using a 2.75 arbor.

5 With the cap installed (not shown), this seal was centered enough to make good lip contact all the way around. We went ahead and used the lip-type main seal in this assembly.

6 The lip seal in this block was way off-center. There was heavy lip contact on the block side and an increasing gap on the cap side. We could have machined material off the cap to try to reduce the uneven gap but installed a self-centering rope-type seal instead.

7 On the crankshaft, the main seal's journal measures 2.812 inches and has a knurled surface. This is intended to allow some oil into the rope-type seal's contact area. The knurl should be polished smooth when using the later neoprene rubber lip seal.

8 A common main seal assembly error is installing the seal insert into the cap with the lip's taper facing in the wrong direction. The high point of the lip seal faces to the inside of the engine and the taper side points outward. What looks right, when looking down at the cap, is wrong when you flip the cap over to install it.

Sealing the Main Seal *CONTINUED*

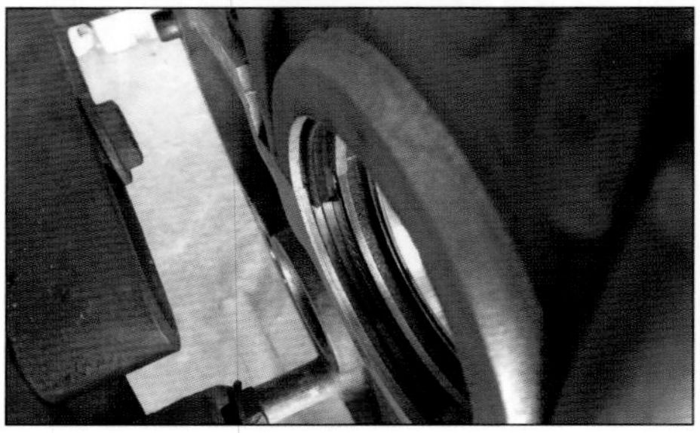

9 ***You can easily see that oil will get past a flipped lip seal insert. To ensure correct assembly once the crankshaft is installed, preassemble the seal to review its alignment and then paint or mark the seal and cap.***

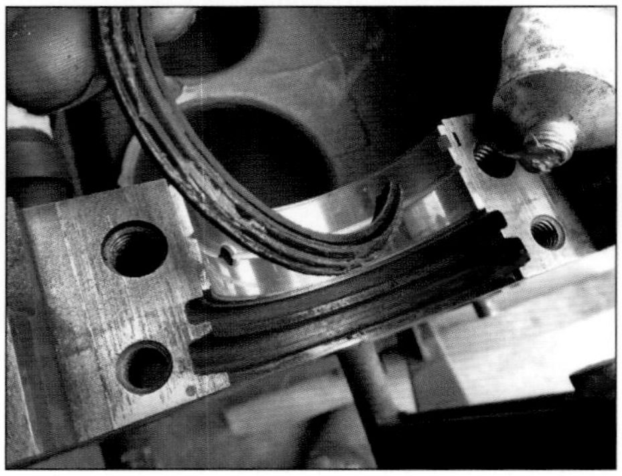

10 ***Apply a small amount of RTV sealer to the backside of the two-piece lip seal to make sure oil does not get around the outside of the seal inserts.***

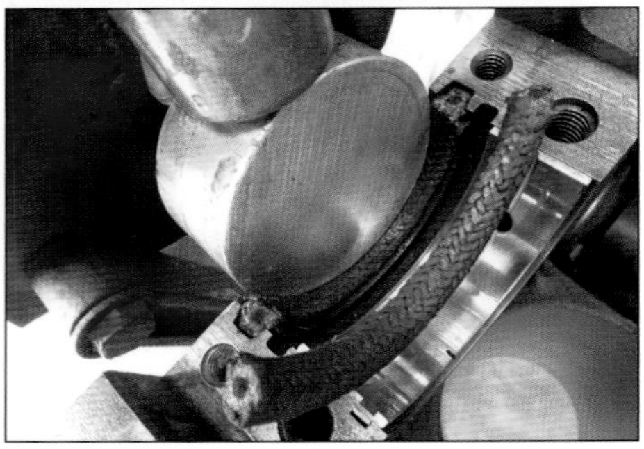

11 ***A rope seal needs to be packed into the receiver grooves and then trimmed to fit. Use a piece of 2¾-inch pipe or some other rounded driver to pack the seal into the groove.***

Crankshaft Installation

Inspect an uninstalled crankshaft in the following areas to be sure it is ready for installation:

Crankshaft Type and Journal Sizes: Are the bearings the correct type, and does the size match the crankshaft's journals? The fastest way to perform this check is by placing one of the number-3 thrust bearing inserts onto the number-3 main bearing journal. The sides of the thrust bearing will either interfere or be loose between the walls of the crank journal if it is the incorrect main bearing for the crank. The back of the bearing will be marked "STD" or with an undersize dimension (0.010, 0.020, etc.) that should match a measurement that you can make with a caliper. The standard main bearing size is 2.750 (STD), so a bearing insert marked 0.010 would have a crank journal that measures 2.740 (2.750 – 0.010).

Torque Converter Counterbore and Pilot Bearing Hole Size: One of the most common areas of confusion and problems when swapping Slant Six crankshafts is the flex plate or flywheel that is attached to the rear of the crank. Verify that the crank you have will mate to the transmission in the vehicle. Do not assume that the crankshaft that came back from the machine shop is the same crank that came out of the engine that came out of your vehicle; we have seen otherwise. Take the time to measure the rear of the crank, to confirm that the shoulder and counterbore are the correct size. Change the pilot bushing in the rear of the crank if the engine is being installed into a manual transmission vehicle. Some early Slant Six crankshafts do not have drilled or finish-machined pilot bushing holes, so inspect for this if needed.

Threaded Holes: Inspect all of the threaded holes to be sure they are clean and in good condition. This is especially important with the 3/4-16 UNF threaded hole in the front of the crank. That hole often gets packed with road dirt and grime. Also check all countersinks to be sure that the fasteners can be started easily. Threaded holes need be clean and should accept the fasteners without any issues. Check and address any threaded hole problems prior to installing the crankshaft.

Keyway and Key: "Make-do" engine assemblers will often use a large crescent or pipe wrench to grip and turn an engine by the front of the crankshaft, but doing this can

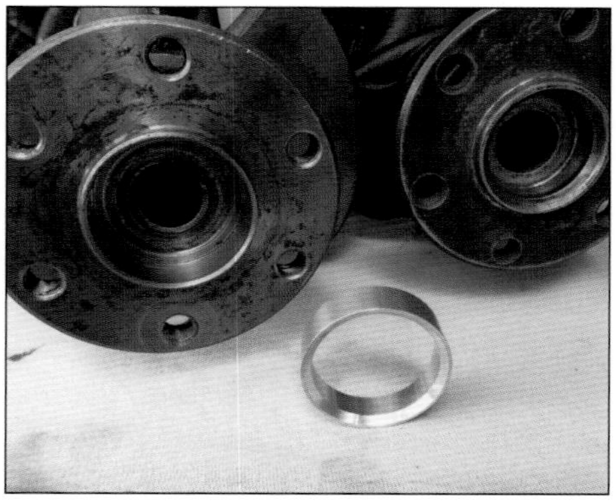

Inspect the rear of the crankshaft to be sure the pilot bearing bore or torque converter counterbore is the correct size. The automatic transmission torque converter support counterbore size was increased in 1968, so a 1967 and older crankshaft with the smaller counterbore will not fit. Use the 0.125-inch wall adapter ring shown if using a later crankshaft or engine with the early torque converter.

damage the front of the crank and the key, making it hard to install the lower timing gear and damper. Inspect the front crankshaft snout to make sure it is undamaged and the keyway and key are in good condition. Crankshaft grinders have to remove the key to do regrinding or crank polishing work and may forget to reinstall the key, so make sure it is not missing.

Oil Cross-Hole Deburr and Cleaning: Inspect the drilled oil feed cross-holes to be sure they are clean and not obstructed. Each cross-hole entry and exit point should be chamfered and smooth. Weld repair or significant crank journal regrinding can obstruct or reduce the hole size, so careful deburring and chamfering may be needed. Always clean these cross-holes with carburetor cleaner and a brush to be sure there is no metal or grinding dust hiding in these holes. Make sure the main caps, the bolts, and the mating cap surfaces on the engine block are clean and free of burrs.

Once all of these items are checked and you can stand the crank on its end, it is time to install the lower timing gear onto the crankshaft. The gear is a 0.001 interference fit. Measure the inner diameter (ID) of the lower gear and the outer diameter (OD) of the crankshaft snout to be sure the interference is not excessive. Sand or hone the gear ID if needed.

Heat the gear to make it easier to slide onto the crank. If the crank is already installed in the engine, use a

Measure the replacement lower timing gear and matching crankshaft journal for the correct interference fit. Set the gear's key and press on the lower timing gear prior to installing the crankshaft into the engine.

3/4-16 UNF bolt and sleeve to draw the gear onto the crankshaft. Install the main seal and the upper grooved main bearing inserts into the engine block, lubricate everything, and install the crankshaft.

Installing the Crankshaft

1 Heat the lower gear to 450 degrees to expand its bore and make installation easier. We use the hub of an old vibration damper as a driver, but a section of pipe also works.

2 If the crankshaft is already installed in the engine, use a 3/4-16 UNF bolt and a sleeve to draw the lower gear onto the crank. Do not pound the gear on with a hammer. Doing so can damage the number-3 main bearing's thrust surfaces.

3 A light pass with a long, fine-tooth flat file is a good way to make sure the main bearing cap surfaces on the block are clean and free of burrs. Run a razor blade over the bearing saddles to be sure those are clean and free of nicks. Wipe up any dirt or metal filings you create.

4 Clean the contact surfaces of the main caps before installing the bearing inserts. Any dirt or nicks between the bearing saddle and insert will impact the oil clearances. Be sure everything is clean and free of burrs, especially along the edges of the saddles.

Installing the Crankshaft *CONTINUED*

5 *Install the main bearing inserts by placing the tab in the notch and pushing the insert into the saddle. The grooved bearings with the oil holes install into the block, and the nongrooved insert goes into the cap. The number-3 position takes the thrust, so that bearing insert looks different from the others.*

6 *The number-3 main bearing position takes the end-to-end crankshaft thrust movement, so that bearing insert has side walls on it. Incorrect cast versus forged crankshaft bearings are obvious at the number-3 thrust position. Install those inserts first to confirm that you have the correct type of bearings for the engine.*

7 *With the timing gear, main seal, upper bearing inserts, and lubrication all in place, install the crankshaft. A Slant Six crank weighs between 65 and 80 pounds, depending on year and type. If needed, get help lifting it. (Photo Courtesy Steve Magnante)*

8 *The crankshaft must drop straight down on the thrust bearing. Take care to watch that position as you lower the unit into position. Give the crank a short spin once it is in place, to be sure that it moves freely.*

9 *A chamfered edge on the number-1 upper main bearing insert allows pressurized oil to shoot onto the timing gear and chain. Install an oil slinger to help distribute some of this oil around the inside the timing chain cover.*

10 *Slant Six main bearing caps have their position number cast into the cap for easy identification. The number-1 cap is at the front of the engine, closest to the timing chain. The number-4 cap is at the rear, next to the main seal. The number-3 cap holds the flanged thrust bearing.*

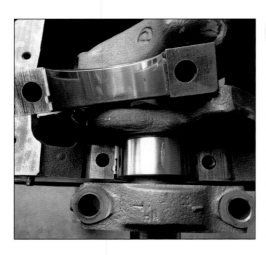

11 *Use 0.002 to 0.006 (red) Plastigauge to check the main bearing clearances. Place some light grease or oil in the crankshaft journal to hold the Plastigauge in place while installing and torquing down, then removing the cap. Do not rotate the crankshaft while doing this check. Note: The casted-in main cap number goes to the camshaft side of the engine and both bearing insert tabs are together on the opposite side (freeze plug side).*

12 *Match the width of the compressed Plastigauge to the guide on the wrapper. The oil clearance is specified between 0.0005 and 0.002. Crankshaft reconditioning (regrinding) is recommended at 0.0025 clearance and/or 0.001 out-of-round journal(s). This used and repolished crankshaft is right at 0.0025 clearance with smooth and round journals, so we decided to use it as is.*

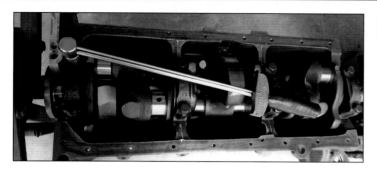

13 Install the lower (ungrooved) main bearing inserts into the caps and carefully install the caps into the recesses on the block. The caps only go on one way, so position the casted-in cap numbers to face the camshaft and group the bearing insert tabs to face the other side. Position the cap above the recess, install the two bolts, and then gently tap the cap straight down so it does not cock to either side. Torque the main cap bolts to 85 ft-lbs before installing the lower rear main seal and cap.

14 Inspect the main seal cap for damage and/or stripped threads. Lightly sand the face where the cap mates to the block to be sure it is flat and free of deep scratches or defects.

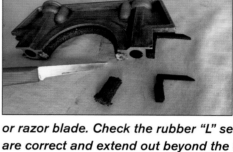

15 Pack the rope seal into the cap the same way as the block side, using a rounded tool. Trim any excess with a sharp knife or razor blade. Check the rubber "L" seals to be sure they are correct and extend out beyond the cap pockets.

16 Trial fit the lower main seal and cap assembly without the rubber L seals to check seal compression and fit. Most Slant Six main seal cap bolts have a 12-point hex-head bolt, so make sure you have the correct 3/8 12-point socket.

17 This rope seal looks good with nice compression and very little fiber getting caught between the cap and block surfaces. Use a small flat-blade screwdriver to push any outlying fibers back into the groove.

18 Apply sealer to the cap surfaces and L seals to hold them in place. A light coat of silicone-based RTV on the rubber L seal faces helps them slide into the opening in the block. Insert the main seal cap assembly by slightly tilting it and starting one L seal and then compressing the other seal, to get it into the block recess.

19 The most overlooked areas are the bolt holes. Apply some sealer to the bolt shoulders and threads to seal that oil pathway.

Installing the Crankshaft *CONTINUED*

20 The main seal cap bolt heads are exposed to the outside of the engine, and the surrounding cap edges prevent access to the number-4 main bearing cap bolt heads when the rear main seal cap is installed. Excess sealer should be visible along all the cap's sealing surfaces. Do not cut off the ends of the rubber L seals extending onto the oil pan rails; those will help seal the oil pan gasket.

22 Weatherstrip adhesive works well for sticking the rubber L seal ends to the cast-iron engine block. Let the glue dry completely before installing the oil pan rail gaskets. Doing this will keep the tab end from slipping out from under the oil pan gasket and creating an oil leak path.

21 Use carburetor cleaner to clean any oil or assembly lubricant out from under and around the L seals. Now is the time to glue these important seal ends to the block's oil pan gasket surface so they will not shift around during oil pan installation.

23 Slant Six main cap bolt holes can break through into the crankshaft's oil feed holes on the camshaft side of the engine. Replacement bolts, provided for windage trays or aftermarket main cap studs, may be longer and can obstruct the oil supply to the crankshaft, leading to bearing failure. OEM bolts have a $2\frac{7}{8}$-inch underhead length with a 1/2-inch diameter main cap locating shoulder just under the hex head. Inspect any replacement fastener for proper length to be sure it does not block the oil supply to the crankshaft.

Timing Chain and Degreeing the Camshaft

The timing gears and chain establish the relationship between piston movement and the valve events. Most of the upgrades we have reviewed so far improve engine durability, but setting correct valve timing has a direct impact on engine performance, economy, and the placement of the power band in the RPM range. It is important to take the time to understand this process and to install the timing components in the correct position.

The Slant Six used a variety of timing chain and gear designs through its production history, but all these parts interchange. The goal is to select the best available parts for your rebuild and install them for maximum performance and longevity.

The best advice for installing timing gears and chain is to spend the time to degree-in the camshaft. Do not simply line up the dots that are stamped onto the gears. We have installed a lot of timing chain sets, and it is sad to report that the marks stamped onto the components rarely

position the camshaft for maximum engine performance. The only special tool that the cam degreeing process shown here requires is a degree wheel, which can be printed off the Internet.

Timing component quality, chain and gear oiling improvements, and methods to control camshaft walk will also be reviewed. Following the steps outlined below will help you make sure that the components installed will be positioned correctly and in a way that ensures a long service life.

Camshaft Degreeing

1 *Chrysler used all-metal timing components in early Slant Six engines. Later engines used a composite top gear that had molded nylon teeth on an aluminum sprocket. Many aftermarket replacement gears were made by a sintered powdered metal process. The lower crankshaft gears can also be machined castings, billet, or sintered powdered metal construction. A factory cast-iron top and bottom gear set is shown here on the left, and aftermarket powdered metal gears are on the right.*

2 *The nylon-aluminum composite top timing gear is found in many Slant Six engines. Factory versions have a hole for the location dowel, and aftermarket units have a large slot. This type of gear works fine in a stock engine but has lower service life. The color of the nylon is a key indicator of its age. The nylon is almost white when molded but darkens and becomes brittle as it gets older. Upper left is a well-used aftermarket top gear with dark nylon teeth.*

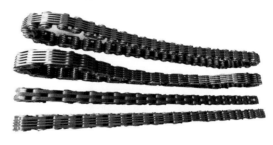

3 *The Slant Six timing chain is offered as link-belt or double roller construction. The more common link-belt chain was made in a variety of ways, by grouping the links in different arrangements. These chains have the same pitch and interchange, but never try to mix and match worn and new parts together.*

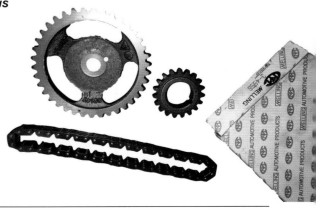

4 *Some aftermarket all-metal timing sets come with a top sprocket that has three wide slots between the hub and the outer gear teeth. This design is okay for stock horsepower engines, but we have seen this type of top gear break at the narrow spokes in high-performance engines.*

Camshaft Degreeing *CONTINUED*

5 We disassemble a lot of Slant Six engines and find the most timing gear wear on the sintered powdered metal gears (center gear). The nylon tooth gears (left) show less wear but have the risk of sudden failure. The early, all-metal original equipment manufacturer (OEM) gears (right) show the least amount of wear in high-mileage engines.

8 The damper is made by pressing an outer ring onto an inner hub with a layer of rubber in between. The TDC timing mark is cut into the outer V-groove ring and can vary in size and placement. Clean the outer ring and look for the factory mark. Once you find the mark, paint it white. Inspect the rubber between the two damper sections to see if it is in good condition. Missing or displaced rubber may indicate that the outer ring has slipped, which will shift the timing mark's position and make the damper wobble.

6 These days you get what you pay for with replacement Slant Six timing chain and gear sets. Spend the time to find OEM parts or spend the money on a premium racing timing chain set. Premium timing chain and gear sets have top and bottom billet-steel gears, adjustable timing, and multiple keyway lower gear with induction-hardened teeth and a double-row roller chain.

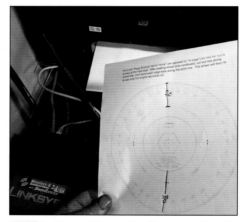

9 You will need a degree wheel. Beg, borrow, buy a "professional" (metal) degree wheel, or print one off of the Internet. The Slant Six damper measures 7 inches, and the wheel we found online printed at that diameter without having to fuss with printer settings.

7 There are two main types of timing marks used on the front of the Slant Six. The early style used a bolt-on timing tab that is viewed from the driver's side. The top dead center (TDC) mark on the matching damper is at the four o'clock position from the key slot. The later timing tab is welded onto the cover and is viewed from the passenger's side of the vehicle. The matching damper has a TDC mark that is slightly shifted to the right of the twelve o'clock key slot. The timing chain cover, the timing tab, and the damper should be kept as a set.

10 Attach the paper degree wheel to the damper with glue or tape. It can also be mounted to thick poster board for a more rigid backing. We simply spray the front of the damper with some adhesive, line up the TDC marks, and stick the paper wheel right to its face.

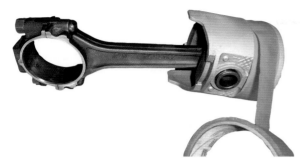

11 The camshaft degreeing trial assembly work is the most complicated mock-up, but it is also the most important one you will do during an engine build. Start by wrapping a single layer of tape around the ring grooves of a piston. Install that piston into the number-6 cylinder using the proper connection rod bearing inserts. Pistons number-1 and number-6 move in unison, so the number-6 piston will give us visual reference to the simultaneous number-1 piston movements as we perform the camshaft position measurements in degrees of rotation. Using a single piston without the rings makes it easier to turn the engine to take the degree readings.

12 Set the engine block straight up on the engine stand and roughly position the camshaft and crankshaft in their TDC positions. The dowel pin in the camshaft needs to be straight up to the deck surface, as does the keyway in the crankshaft. Use a carpenter's square and reference the number-6 piston to help find these TDC locations.

13 Check the camshaft (top) chain sprocket for an oil drain hole. This hole will keep oil pressure from building up behind the sprocket, pushing the camshaft forward, and changing the gear mesh relationship at the oil pump gear. The hole also transfers oil out to the face of the sprocket, where it is thrown onto the chain and around the inside of the timing cover. If the chain sprocket doesn't have a hole, add one by drilling a 1/8 inch or larger through hole from the outer edge of the mounting pocket to the front face of the gear.

14 Install the gear, chain, timing chain cover, and damper with the degree wheel. Start the damper onto the crankshaft snout keyway just enough to turn the crankshaft and reference the degree wheel marks to the timing tab. These parts will be removed and reinstalled a few times during the cam degreeing process, so only install a couple of snug bolts to hold down the cover and use a light set on the damper to make disassemblies easier.

Camshaft Degreeing CONTINUED

15 Timing parts are installed, and our paper degree wheel is ready to take some readings. Also install two lifters, the cylinder head, two pushrods in the number-1 cylinder position, and the rocker arm assembly so you can watch the valve movements.

16 With the front engine block deck dowel pin removed, install the cylinder head so the number-2 combustion chamber is over cylinder bore number-1. Doing this head offset partially exposes the number-6 cylinder and piston assembly that was installed earlier. Use four head bolts around the number-1 cylinder and two more at the rear of the engine and snug them down. There is no need to use a head gasket or torque the bolts if the deck surfaces are clean and flat.

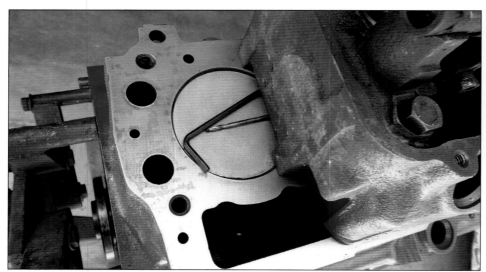

17 The staggered head installation makes an easy positive stop so true TDC can be found. Find a piece of metal that is 0.010- to 0.020-inch thicker than the measured deck height and place it on the center of the piston between the head and piston top. Incremental drill bits or Allen wrenches work well as a convenient insert. Rotate the crankshaft until it stops on the insert. Mark that location on the timing tab, remove the insert, rotate the crank to the other side of TDC, and repeat the process. The timing tab's zero (0) mark should be centered between the two new marks you created.

18 Our timing tab was off by about 3 degrees, so we adjusted its location by bending it. Wipe off your original marks (use a different colored marker) to do a recheck. The valve events can be checked once true TDC has been determined and the valve lash is set to the cam card's specifications.

19 Degreeing the cam confirms that the valves are opening and closing per the camshaft's design, which is listed on the cam card. Set the valve clearance (lash) to the specifications listed on the card. Factory Slant Six camshaft lash settings are 0.010 inch for the intake valves and 0.020 inch for the exhaust. Rotate the engine and watch the valve movements, then use your fingers to rotate the pushrod to find the exact point where the lash disappears and the valve starts to open. Mark your degree wheel at those points.

20 This cam checked well with the overlap event centered over TDC, exhaust opening at 120 degrees ATDC, and the intake valve closing at 60 degrees ABDC. The intake valve closing point (IC) is the most important event because that directly impacts the engine's effective (running) compression ratio. Use the IC number you find here to calculate your engine's effective compression ratio.

21 Slant Six engines respond well to valve timing advance, so we advanced this cam 2 degrees to improve our effective compression result and offset future valve timing retard from timing chain stretch and component wear. Drilling out the dowel pin hole and shimming the camshaft forward (clockwise) did the trick. There is an offset bushing kit available; use that kit if you need to move the cam more than just a couple of degrees.

22 Do the final installation once the cam degreeing work is complete. Clean the threads in the front of the camshaft and be sure to use the original hardened retaining bolt and beveled washer to fasten the cam sprocket to the cam. This bolt and spring washer combination is engineered to take a lot of vibration and load, so do not replace them with parts of unknown quality. We used a small drop of Loctite on the bolt threads and torqued the bolt to 40 ft-lbs to reduce the chance of it loosening.

23 Slant Six engines have an oil slinger that gets sandwiched between the lower timing sprocket and the hub of the vibration damper. The slinger acts as a backstop and thrower of oil that comes out of the chamfer along the tab side of the number-1 upper main bearing insert (white arrow). Many rebuilt Slant Sixes we see have dry and worn-out timing components because the factory's method for oiling these parts was eliminated or not used to begin with.

Static and Effective Compression Calculators

There are calculators available online that will help you determine your compression ratio. You will need a few measurements to calculate static and effective (dynamic or running) compression in a Slant Six. We've listed some common values, or a range of values, for those measurements. Where a range is listed, measure your engine to find an actual value.

The hardest number to find (and the most important) is the intake valve's closing point (IC). That value should be obtained by mocking up the valvetrain and checking the intake valve's closing point with the actual valve clearance (lash) set.

The IC and the effective compression ratio number become especially important when an aftermarket performance camshaft is used. A static compression increase is usually needed to get acceptable effective compression and the corresponding performance gains from the new cam. Target 8:1 effective compression for engines using regular pump gas and up to 8.4:1 for premium pump fuel and/or when using an octane booster. ∎

Cylinder Head Volume	50 cc to 60 cc
Piston Head Volume	0 (zero) cc
Head Gasket Thickness	0.020 inch to 0.060 inch
Head Gasket Bore Size	3.50 inches to 3.60 inches
Deck Clearance to Piston	− 0.100 inch to − 0.200 inch*
Slant Six Strokes	170 at 3.125 inches 198 at 3.640 inches 225 at 4.125 inches
Connecting Rod Length	170 at 5.7 inches 198 at 7.0 inches 225 at 6.7 inches
Intake Valve Closing	40 degrees to 80 degrees ABDC**

* Some online calculators enter a negative deck clearance value as a positive number.
** ABDC = After Bottom Dead Center

Connecting Rod, Piston, and Ring Set Preparation

Factory Slant Six pistons and connecting rods use an interference fit, pressed-in piston pin. Special equipment is needed for assembly, so assembly work is best done by an automotive machine shop with that equipment. Floating piston pins are found in some aftermarket performance pistons, and that setup can easily be assembled at home with basic hand tools.

Most piston pins are offset in the piston by 1/16 inch toward the major thrust side (camshaft side) of the engine. The offset is done to reduce piston slap, so check your piston and rod assemblies to make sure the pistons are assembled onto the connecting rods in the correct orientation. The pin offset impacts piston speeds around TDC and BDC, connecting rod bearing loads, and internal engine friction. Do not reverse the piston with the notches facing rearward instead of forward in hopes of reducing friction.

Piston rings come in a variety of designs, but they all assemble onto the pistons in the same way. Start with the oil ring and then work your way up the piston. The biggest concerns with piston ring installation are making sure that everything is clean, that the rings and their gaps are correct for the bore size, and that the rings are installed in the correct piston groove position with the top side of the ring facing the correct way.

Preparing the Rods, Pistons, and Ring Set

1 *Most Slant Six pistons have an offset piston pin to help reduce piston noise. The pin is closer to the camshaft side of the engine when the notch on the piston top is facing forward. Measure from the piston pin to the sides of the piston to figure out how much offset there is and which side of the piston it is on.*

2 *Typical piston to connecting rod assembly aims the connecting rod's oil spurt hole toward the camshaft and the notch on the piston facing the front of the engine. Later cast-crankshaft Slant Six connecting rods have the oil spurt hole in a different location (near the beam of the connecting rod), but it still points toward the major thrust side of the engine.*

3 *We sometimes see sticky or gulled-up piston pins, especially in tall-block (RG) Slant Six engines. Factory pistons relied on pin bore oil clearance to get the oil to the pin, while aftermarket replacement pistons have additional holes or slots that allow more oil into the pin to piston contact area. Racing pistons have oil feed holes connecting the pin bore to the oil ring groove, so the pin gets pressurized oil. Slots or holes use oil mist and splash to lubricate the pin, so consider drilling some pin oiling holes if the replacement pistons do not already have them.*

4 *Used pistons need to be inspected for skirt and ring groove wear and completely cleaned, especially inside the ring grooves. New replacement pistons should be checked for proper size and uniform weights prior to assembling them onto the connecting rods. No matter how clean the piston and connecting rod assemblies look after returning from the machine shop, perform a final soap and water cleaning on them prior to installing the ring sets.*

Preparing the Rods, Pistons, and Ring Set CONTINUED

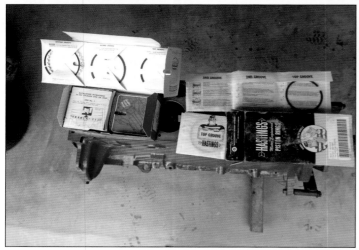

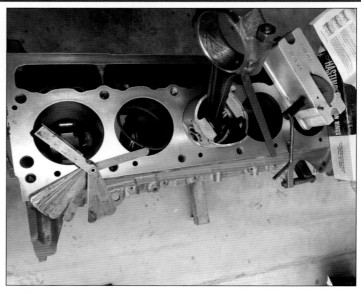

5 There are a variety of ring sets available, but plain cast-iron rings work well in most any Slant Six. Purchase your ring set with the pistons to ensure the sizes match and that the cylinder bore honing finish is compatible with the ring material being used. Pay careful attention to the packaging containing the ring set because each ring's groove position, orientation, and other instructions are often printed directly on the boxes or sleeves containing the rings. Work with one ring at a time and keep everything organized to prevent mix-ups.

6 Check the ring gaps by inserting a ring into the bore and using an upside-down piston as a driver to square the ring. Use a thickness gauge to find the size of the gap. We have a fancy ring gap grinding tool to quickly open up tight gaps, but a fine-tooth flat file also adjusts and/or deburrs the gaps. Work with one ring at a time and install it directly onto the piston or place it back into the correct packaging, once the gap is set.

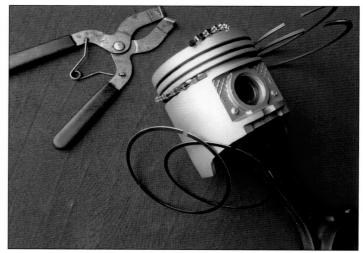

7 The compression ring gaps should be 0.010 inch to 0.020 inch and uniform from the bore wall to the inner edge of the ring. This gap measured 0.012 inch right out of the box, so it is good to use as is. Pay attention to stamped marks or features on the rings that show which side is up. This ring has a small dot on its side that faces to the top of the engine. Some rings have a step or a bevel on an edge that indicates its correct orientation.

8 There are five rings total per piston. Two are compression rings, and three make up the oil ring assembly. Start with the lowest groove, which contains the oil ring. Install the wide expander first, being sure that the ends do not overlap each other. Use the two thin rails along the upper and lower edges of the expander to lock it in place.

9 *Install the number-2 compression ring into the second ring groove. This ring had a bevel in the inner bottom edge and a dot on the top surface of the ring. The top ring goes on last. It has a bevel on the upper, inner edge and a dot on the top surface. We have some special ring pliers, but we prefer to set the piston's connecting rod end into the block's lifter pocket, to hold it, then spread open and install the rings with our fingers.*

Piston, Rod, and Bearing Installation

Installing the piston and connecting rod assemblies is a straightforward process that repeats itself six times. This important task requires the use of a ring compressor, three different lubricants, and a critical sequence of steps that needs to be repeated in a consistent fashion. Get organized and have everything ready to go before installing the first piston assembly.

There are two steps that are critical to a successful engine rebuild: orientation of the piston notch to the front of the engine and getting the connecting rod caps installed correctly (bearing tabs and numbers together). Pay close attention to those steps. Most pistons have a built-in offset to help reduce piston noise, so check to see if the pistons have this feature. Also check to see if they were all hung on the connecting rods correctly. Connecting rods are finish honed to final size with the cap installed and torqued to specification, so a flipped cap does not position the connecting rod bearing inserts correctly and leads to fast rod bearing failure.

Staggering the piston ring gaps around the piston head and making sure the cylinder bore and ring packs are well lubricated prior to piston installation is important. There are a number of different ways to space the ring gaps around the piston head, but the most important issue is keeping the compression ring gaps from lining up with each other. We go another step and position the compression ring gaps in a way that is helpful in an engine that is slanted 30 degrees to one side. Piston rings do have some weight, and they will drift a little until they seat in the bores, so make sure you place the gaps away from each other as much as possible.

Lubricants

Engine assembly lubrication (or assembly lube) takes many forms. It can be a high-viscosity oil that comes in a bottle or a thick grease that is packaged in a tube or tub. We prefer the thicker types because they are easier to apply and the grease stays where you put it, even if the new engine sits for a while before starting.

Many engines have been successfully assembled and lived long service lives by using plain motor oil. For engine assembly, a thick (high-viscosity) single-weight oil is the preferred lubrication to use on freshly honed cylinders, new piston rings, and the timing chain.

Molybdenum disulfide (or moly lube) is a dark gray to black high-pressure grease that contains $MoS2$ to provide boundary lubrication properties. This is a fancy term that means the lubricant is absorbed into the microscopic pores of the contacting surfaces to provide better high-load wear protection. Moly lube is used on camshaft lobes, gear tooth contact surfaces, and fastener threads where pure hydrodynamic film lubricants do not provide enough protection. Use moly lubricants sparingly and only on high-load surfaces because it also sticks and plugs the "pores" inside the oil filter.

Vaseline is an item that is sometimes used in automotive engine rebuilding, mostly to prime the oil pump so it develops immediate suction. Vaseline will dissolve quickly into the motor oil, but it has lower lubricity and should be used sparingly.

Tools and Parts Needed

- Pistons, ring pack, and connecting rod assembly
- Ring compressor
- 9/16 socket wrench
- Torque wrench
- Thickness gauge
- Rod bolt protectors
- Plastigauge for 0.001 to 0.003 (green)
- Connecting rod bearings
- Assembly lubricant
- Engine oil
- Molybdenum disulfide paste for the bolt threads
- Soft driver to tap the assemblies into their bores

Installing the Pistons, Rods, and Bearings

1 The connecting rods and pistons (with the ring packs installed) are ready and waiting for installation. We mark the cylinder position on all the rods and piston heads and caps, and then we remove the caps. The most common ring compressor available is an adjustable spring steel sleeve. There is also a clamping plier-type tool available that is a little faster to use.

2 Rotate the engine block onto its side so there is access to the bore tops and the crankshaft journals. We put the driver's side (freeze plug side) up so the lifter gallery is below the bores. This side of the block provides a large, flat surface to put stuff on. This orientation places the connection rod's oil spurt hole, bearing tabs, and stamped number out of view; if you need more visual reference points as a guide to correct assembly, put the other side of the block up.

3 The connecting rod bearing tabs and connecting rod numbers are easier to view with the passenger's side of the engine block facing up. Use the block orientation that works best for you. It is a good idea to cover the oil pump and fuel pump openings if you leave the block in this position for an extended period of time.

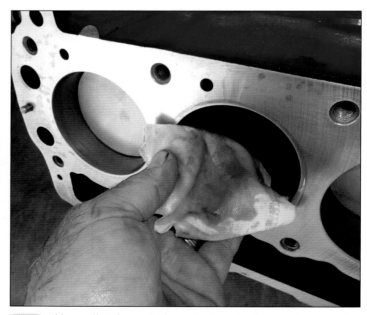

4 Use a lint-free cloth and wipe the bores down with engine oil. Wet the cylinder walls top to bottom to ensure that they are well lubricated and clean prior to installing the connecting rod, piston, and rings.

5 *Stagger the ring gaps. The top ring gap points to the driver's side, the second ring gap 180 degrees away to the passenger's side. Space the oil ring gaps at 120-degree intervals and not in line with the two compression ring gaps above. This orientation places the top gap at the highest point of the slanted cylinder so any liquid entering the bore does not migrate into the ring pack. The low second ring gap lets trapped liquid out. Oil the rings, then compress them, install the upper bearing insert into the rod, and lubricate the bearing and the threads of the rod bolts. Install bolt protection sleeves to ensure that the crankshaft journal(s) do not get damaged during installation.*

6 *Position the crankshaft so a pair of connecting rod journals are away from the bores. Place that piston assembly into the corresponding bore with the notch on the piston top facing forward. Tap the assembly into the bore with a soft driver until the piston clears the tool and is down in the bore. Set the ring compressor aside at this point to free up a hand.*

7 *Continue tapping on the piston head while you guide the connecting rod and bearing onto the crankshaft journal with your other hand. Look for an adjacent crankshaft counterweight that has a long, flat side. Push or twist the connecting rod's side against that flat. This aligns the connecting rod to the crank journal's bearing surface as you tap the assembly down into the bore.*

8 *Keep the rod centered over the journal as it gets close so the bearing insert does not shift out of position. There will be a solid-sounding* klunk *when the bearing contacts the journal surface. Remove the bolt protectors and get the matching connecting rod cap and retaining nuts.*

Installing the Pistons, Rods, and Bearings CONTINUED

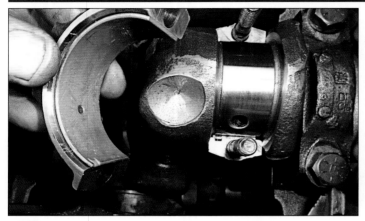

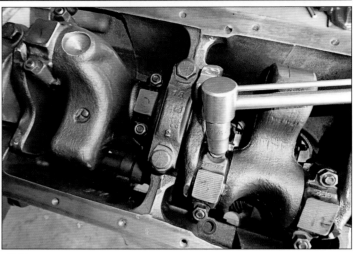

9 Install the rod bearing insert into the cap and grease it with engine assembly lubricant. Many engine builders use engine oil here, but we prefer something thicker so the lubricant stays in place over time. Match up the bearing tabs and the stamped numbers on the outside of the connection rod, then push the cap onto the bolts. The tabs and numbers all face the camshaft in most applications. The cap will slide onto the rod bolts easily if everything is orientated correctly.

10 Lubricate and install the connecting rod cap retaining nuts. Tighten them down evenly until they are snug and everything is seated. Torque the nuts to 45 ft-lbs using a 9/16 socket. We like to torque the connecting rod nuts in two steps: first take both nuts to 20 ft-lbs while feeling for clearance and then complete the tightening to 45 ft-lbs.

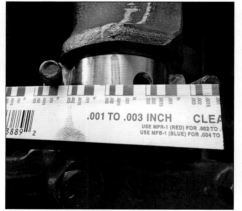

11 Perform a preliminary bearing clearance check by pushing the rod side to side in the journal. There should be some slight movement within the side clearance between the connecting rod and the sides of the crankshaft journal. Twist the assembly as you move it to help force excess assembly grease out of the way. If there is no movement, remove the cap and inspect for nicks, contamination, or incorrect cap to rod orientation. Once you feel movement, rotate the crankshaft a couple of revolutions, taking note of the increased resistance from the piston and rings you just installed.

12 Check the exact bearing clearance with Plastigauge. Set a strip of the Plastigauge onto the journal, install and torque the cap to spec, then remove the cap. The connecting rod bearing oil clearance is called out between 0.0005 and 0.002. This journal was at 0.0015, so it is okay. Do not rotate the crank or wiggle the rod cap in the side clearance while doing this check. Clean off all the Plastigauge once finished.

13 Inspect the connecting rod to crankshaft rod journal side clearances by using a thickness gauge inserted into the slight gap between the parts. The factory clearance is between 0.007 to 0.012. A slightly wider side clearance is okay, but less clearance is risky. Increased side friction and reduced oil flow through and out of the bearing area can lead to overheating and early bearing failure.

CYLINDER HEAD ASSEMBLY

The Slant Six cylinder head has the advantage of being a 12-port head (individual ports for each valve). The main disadvantage of the design is the long, curved port shape that is created by the engine's 30-degree slant. Another disadvantage is that the cylinder head's port and valve size were calculated and produced based on the original 170-ci engine size, which means the head is "flow limited" as the engine's cubic inch size and/or the operating RPM range increases.

Cylinder head refurbishment to increase flow requires special tools and knowledge. Most beginner engine builders have head rebuilding work done by an experienced machine shop. You can save money and improve performance if you do some of the disassembly, preparation, and parts procurement yourself. A valve spring compressor is needed to disassemble a cylinder head. That tool can be rented or borrowed from most machine shops or auto parts stores.

Removing the Valves and Springs

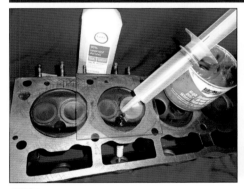

1 Measure the combustion chamber sizes in the cylinder heads before removing the valves. Use a clear plastic plate with two holes drilled in it and a large syringe (60 cc minimum). Install a spark plug, seal the plate to the head surface with grease, and fill the chamber with fluid (we use alcohol). Write down this measurement (in cubic centimeters) because it is needed to calculate static and effective compression ratios.

2 The valve and spring are held in place by the spring retainer and keepers. Retention relies on a collating action that jams the parts together into a tapered bore. Before attempting to compress the valve springs, use a hammer to hit the edge of each retainer to loosen the tight fit between the parts.

3 The valve spring compressor is basically a large C clamp that pushes on the valve head and the retainer, compressing the spring. Adjust the spread of the fork end so it grips the spring retainer tightly and change the travel distance so the tool locks when the valve spring is fully compressed.

Removing the Valves and Springs CONTINUED

4 *Remove the two keeper halves from the grooves in the valve stem. Keep in mind that exhaust valves have three grooves and intake valves have two, so the keepers are different. Release the compressor once the keepers are out. The valve spring with retainer will now be loose. Remove the rubber valve stem seal by sliding it up and off the end of the valve stem or just break it off the stem if the seal is brittle.*

5 *Used valves will often have "pounded" stem tips and/or sharp, raised edges around the keeper grooves. These will prevent the valve from passing through the valve guide. Use a flat file to remove those protruding edges so the valve slides through the guide easily and does not damage or scratch it as the stem grooves pass through.*

6 *The Slant Six valve stems have 3/8-inch diameters and two types of valve stem seals. The rubber push-on stem seal slides onto the protruding top of the valve guide, allowing the valve's stem to move through its fixed position sealing area. The umbrella-type stem seal grips the valve stem and moves with it, touching the top of the valve guide at full valve lift. Both types of stem seal work well, but the push-on style tends to wear out faster.*

Inspecting Valve Seats and Guides

The main difference with Slant Six cylinder head castings is the use of spark plug tubes. Decide if you prefer the later no spark plug tube "peanut plug" head casting prior to starting any head work. The later no-tubes head is less likely to leak oil, and all of these heads came from the factory with induction-hardened exhaust valve seats.

The typical wear points for cylinder heads include the valve seats, valve guides, rocker arm assembly, and valves themselves. Review these areas so you can discuss any concerns with the machine shop that will be doing the rebuilding work.

This discussion will help you estimate the cost of the valve job. This inspection work is especially important if you have a few different heads to choose from and want or need to purchase your own parts. For the best value, focus your efforts on rebuilding a preferred cylinder head casting that needs the least amount of repair work.

Valve Seat and Guide Inspection

1 *The 1960 through 1975 Slant Six heads used spark plug tubes and had a revised combustion chamber design starting in 1968. Nontube heads were introduced in 1977, eliminating a common source of oil leaks. Other changes made to the head during its production run included induction-hardened valve seats and air injection ports. Decide which casting is best for you prior to rebuilding heads.*

Valve Seat and Guide Inspection *CONTINUED*

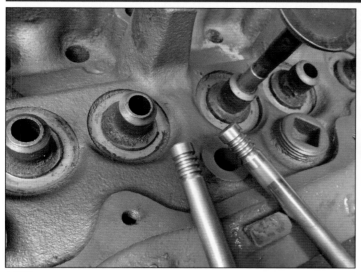

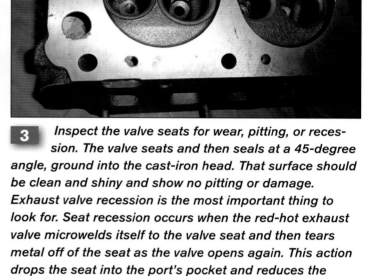

2 *Check for excessive valve guide wear by inserting an upside-down valve from the top of the guide and wiggling it in the oil clearance. There should be just a slight amount of side-to-side movement. Review the grooves and the tip of the valve stem for wear. The "lands" between the grooves wear and get thin, and the tip can get pitted and mushroomed. The body of the stem will wear undersize, showing shiny spots or a step where the stem meets the valve guide. Replace any valves that show this type of wear.*

3 *Inspect the valve seats for wear, pitting, or recession. The valve seats and then seals at a 45-degree angle, ground into the cast-iron head. That surface should be clean and shiny and show no pitting or damage. Exhaust valve recession is the most important thing to look for. Seat recession occurs when the red-hot exhaust valve microwelds itself to the valve seat and then tears metal off of the seat as the valve opens again. This action drops the seat into the port's pocket and reduces the valve's lash clearance at the rocker arm. A receded exhaust valve will appear lower in the chamber and will have a square shouldered seat edge. Replacement seats can be used to repair the damage, but that work adds cost to the cylinder head rebuild.*

4 *Intake valves can also be recessed into the head chamber and port pocket (far right). The main cause is usually excessive or repeated valve and/or valve seat grinding. A valve that is sunk does not flow well, so inspect the head for this condition. Recessed intake valves should be replaced with ones that have oversize heads, so the contact seat can move out and upward.*

5 *Inspect the rocker arm tips for wear. The contact mark should be smooth, shiny, and well centered on the tip radius. Tips that have a slight depression at the contact point can be resurfaced. Rocker arms with tips that are pitted or have a deep contact depression should be replaced.*

Deburring, Oil Drainback, Milling, and Porting

As with the block, the Slant Six cylinder head benefits from some rebuilding preparation work. The finished head provides improved performance and durability. Common sense casting cleanup grinding work along with milling the head gasket surface for flatness and to increase compression are the areas of concern. This work yields significant benefits.

We will review the minimum head work performed on every Slant Six engine we rebuild, but additional porting work combined with oversized valves yields big performance improvements. Time spent on increasing effective compression and improving cylinder head flow has a direct impact on engine performance and economy, especially with a larger-displacement Slant Six.

Cleaning Up the Imperfections

1 *Solid lifter Slant Six engines require occasional valve lash adjustments. This adjustment is best performed hot, on a running engine. Adding oil drainback holes at the lower corners of the head (red tube) and grooves under the lower cylinder head bolts helps direct the "top end" oil into the pushrod openings. The oil then returns to the crankcase while doing lash adjustments. Do not bother with this oil return modification if you have a 1981 or newer Slant Six equipped with hydraulic lifters or if you adjust the valve lash when the engine is not running.*

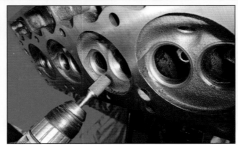

2 *There is a sharp edge where the head port meets the machined angles leading up to the valve seat. The valve seat machining starts with a 15-degree lead-in angle at the combustion chamber. Then there is a 45-degree seat that the valve contacts followed by a 60-degree cut under that surface that transitions into the raw port casting. Remove the sharp edge at that transition point and smooth out the valve pocket area. Grinding away the sharp edge between the 60-degree cut and the raw port casting opens up the passage and improves port flow.*

3 *A close-up view of the sharp edges where the factory machining transitions into the raw casting in the head ports. These edges should be ground away to reduce turbulence and improve airflow. This unported head shows port size reduction and excess material around the valve guides where the transition from machined surface to raw casting occurs.*

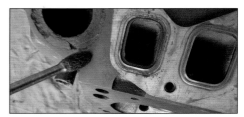

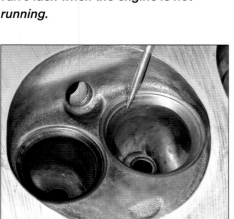

4 *Books have been written on cylinder head porting, but the general cleanup work done on this head shows how the sharp edges under the valve seats have been removed and the material around the valve guide hole has been thinned out. The chambers can also be deburred and relieved at the outer edges of the valves to reduce potential hot spots and improve airflow into the cylinders. (Photo Courtesy Steve Magnante)*

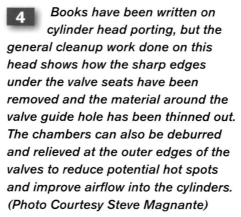

5 *Use the intake and exhaust manifold gaskets to review the port openings in the head. Break sharp edges and remove casting flaws and flash that could interfere with airflow through the port. Manifold ports that are slightly smaller than the head ports are preferred because they help keep fuel in suspension as the air and fuel mixture moves through the manifold runners and into the cylinders.*

Valve Guide, Seat, and Grinding Work

Valve seat and valve face grinding is the main valve job activity. This work is done with special equipment, and there are different levels of quality to be aware of. A low-cost valve job has the machine shop taking the head apart, cleaning the parts, grinding the valve-to-head contact surfaces (seats), and reassembling the head with new valve stem seals. This simple valve job is okay if the head has little to no wear and is being used on a stock engine, but that is seldom the case.

Most Slant Six heads have lots of miles on them and have worn-out valves, recessed valve seats, worn guides, and clogged rocker arms that will need attention and/or replacement. Head resurfacing (milling) increases compression and additional porting work, back-cutting the valves, and performing three-angle seat grinding and cutting improves head flow. This specialized work increases performance and efficiency, so decide if you want to spend extra money to have this additional work done.

Another thing to keep in mind is the valve guides on a Slant Six head were designed to support valve lifts in the 0.400- to 0.450-inch valve lift range (0.260 to 0.300 cam lobe lift). The tops of the guides will need to be trimmed down if you plan to install a high-lift camshaft.

Grinding the Valve Guide and Seat

1 The tops of the factory valve guides will need to be trimmed down if a camshaft with valve lift over 0.450 inch is used in the engine. Aftermarket automotive tool suppliers have special cutters available to do this work, but careful use of a disc grinder will also accomplish the task. The goal is to provide room between the top of the guide and the bottom of the valve spring retainer, when the valve is full open (full lift). Make allowance for the valve stem seal so it does not get crushed between the valve guide and spring retainer.

2 Grinding the bottom of the spring retainers is another place to gain some clearance for a higher lift camshaft. Many of the stamped spring retainers have an uneven surface that can be squared up to gain additional room between the top of the valve guide and the spring retainer.

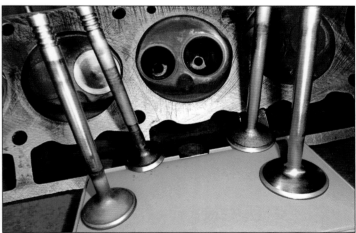

3 Many replacement valves have a step where the 45-degree seat angle ends and intersects the back surface of the valve head. This transition step can be ground off in a process called back-cutting. Many performance valves are already back-cut and the backs of the valve heads are polished to reduce turbulence and carbon buildup. This additional machine work is more important on the intake valves.

Grinding the Valve Guide and Seat CONTINUED

4 A do-it-yourself valve back-cut can be done by chucking the valve in a drill to spin it and then grinding the backside of the valve head with an angle grinder. The forward valve shows the step you want to grind off. The larger valve on the right is an aftermarket oversize Slant Six intake valve that is already back-cut and polished. The other valves show how you can quickly remove the step off a factory valve to improve airflow.

Valve Reinstalling

1 Factory Slant Six valve springs can be reused if they are not broken or worn out. A quick visual check is done by standing all of the springs next to each other and looking for any that have a different height. Springs that are square and measure 2 inches tall are within specifications.

2 Factory valve springs should measure $1\frac{5}{8}$ to $1\frac{11}{16}$ when compressed and installed. Measure between the cylinder head surface and the bottom of the spring retainer with the valve closed to get the exact height. Spring pressure should be 75 pounds with the valve seated and 170 pounds at full lift (stock cam). Spring shims can be used to adjust the spring pressure as needed, but stiffer valve springs should be used with any performance camshaft.

3 Clean and lubricate the valves using engine oil. Squirt oil into the valve guide and onto the seat and then install the valve. Work the valve up and down to be sure it is well oiled and moves freely. Do not use heavy grease or moly lube inside the valve guides; those lubricants do not wash out easily and can cause the valve to stick in the guide.

Valve Reinstalling *CONTINUED*

4 *Install the valve stem seals with the cupped side facing down. Umbrella-type seals have a long-sided version for the intake valves and a short-sided version for the exhaust valves. The shorter seal allows more oil to get into the hotter-running exhaust valve guide.*

5 *Compress the valve spring and retainer over the valve stem and install the keepers. Factory keepers are different between the intake and exhaust valves, so do not mix them up. Place a little grease in the keeper grooves to stick the keeper in place while you release and remove the spring compressor.*

6 *There were different valve springs retainers used over the years. The early ones have a cupped top and the later retainers were completely flat across the top. Using the cupped type on the exhaust valves directs more oil down those valve stems to help with valve lubrication and cooling. Using the flat retainers on the intake valves provides visual distinction that is helpful when doing valve lash adjustments.*

Cylinder Head Assembly

Assembling the cylinder head is a straightforward process. It relies on proper valve stem to guide clearances, correct valve spring pressure, and installed spring heights, which should have been set by the machine shop. Attention to cleanliness and proper lubrication of the parts installed are the areas where the assembler needs to focus.

The rocker arm assembly has specific inspection steps and assembly needs, such as ensuring that the oil passages are clear and valve to rocker arm contact is correct. Be sure the oil holes drilled into the rocker arm shaft are in the correct position, so oil makes its way out to the valve guides and down the pushrods.

FINAL LONG-BLOCK ENGINE ASSEMBLY

The long-block assembly brings all of the parts back together so the engine can be reinstalled into the vehicle. The engine assembly sequence of operations is important because parts can block or make the next assembly operation more difficult. For example, the freeze plugs need to be installed before the manifold assembly, the lifters need to go in before the cylinder head goes on, and the oil pan should be in place before the vibration damper is installed.

The cylinder head and valve gear installation is the most technical aspect of this phase of assembly; preparation and installation of the intake and exhaust manifolds follows as a close second. Installing and getting a good seal on the engine plugs, sheet metal covers, oil pan, and pumps is also important. Proper head gasket and manifold sealing is key to good performance and a smooth running engine. Leak-free oil pan, covers, and accessories keep the new engine looking good and your driveway clean.

Sheet Metal Installation

The sheet metal parts that need to be installed on the long-block include the timing chain cover, the oil pan, and the valve cover. These parts should have been cleaned by the machine shop, but be sure to inspect them for damage and dimpled bolt holes prior to installation.

Sealing is the main concern with these parts. Careful preparation combined with proper seal and/or gasket installation is needed to prevent

Installing the Timing Cover

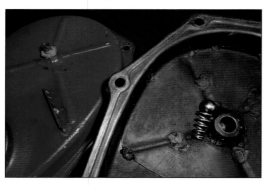

1 The Slant Six does not have a camshaft retaining plate; instead, it relies on the pulling action of the oil pump drive gear and a slight amount of cam lobe taper to keep the camshaft in position. Many engine builders add a thrust button into the timing chain cover to prevent the camshaft from moving forward. Welding a nut to the timing chain cover and using a rocker arm ball-screw is a common technique, but there are a few other ways to prevent the cam from moving forward and out of the block.

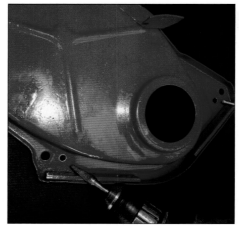

2 The front main seal (timing chain cover oil seal) needs to be well centered on the matching crankshaft journal surface in order to seal well. Ream the dowel pin holes slightly oversize to allow some cover float. This allows the seal and timing chain cover assembly to center itself during cover installation.

Installing the Timing Cover *CONTINUED*

3 *The front seal assembly has a metal outer ring that presses into a recess in the timing chain cover. Most replacement seals have a narrow shoulder that is easily bent, so you may need to make a special driver that reaches down and contacts the base of the seal during assembly. We made our driver out of plastic plumbing pipe.*

6 *A correctly installed oil seal has the outer rubber lip of the seal set straight and flush to the front of the cover. This timing chain cover and oil seal assembly is ready for installation.*

4 *Apply a light coat of gasket sealer to the outer ring of the front oil seal. This prevents oil from leaking around the seal's metal jacket and the sheet metal timing chain cover.*

7 *Apply gasket sealer to the engine block surface and use it to hold the timing chain cover gasket in position. We like to leave the cover side of the gasket dry so that the gasket sticks to the block only and the cover comes off clean if removed later. Install the oil slinger with the cupped side facing forward, and be sure to apply some grease to the rubber seal lip before putting the cover in place.*

9 *The timing chain cover retaining bolt hole located at the water pump to block opening is a threaded through hole into the water jacket. Apply some sealer to this bolt's threads to prevent coolant from seeping through. Be sure to use the correct-length bolt in this position because a longer fastener will extend into the water jacket and hit the number-1 cylinder wall that is located behind this hole.*

5 *Set the cover on a hard surface and tap the seal into the cover's recess with your special driver. Tap different sides of the driver until the seal bottoms out in the pocket, watching to make sure the seal goes straight into the pocket. Wipe off any excess sealer once the seal is in place.*

8 *Position the timing chain cover on the dowel pins and start a couple of bolts to hold the cover in place. Install the vibration damper's hub into the front oil seal and push the cover assembly around on the gasket face, feeling for some movement. We have a broken-off damper hub with a split along the keyslot that easily slides onto the crankshaft and allows close-up viewing of the seal's contact lip to ensure even lip compression all the way around the seal. Install and tighten the remaining cover bolts once everything is centered.*

Installing the Oil Pan

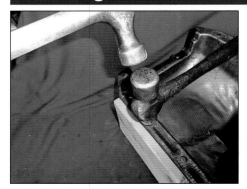

1 *Check the oil pan for damage and distorted bolt holes. Now is the time to knock out any dents in the sump and to repair dimpled bolt holes. Use a ball-peen hammer as a driver and a block of wood to support around the bolt hole. Use another hammer to strike the other end of the ball-peen hammer until the hole is flush with the pan's rail. This technique also works to repair distorted timing chain and valve cover bolt holes.*

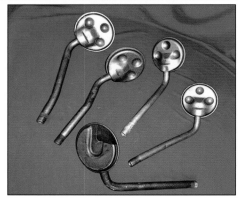

2 *The oil pickup tube moves oil from the pan's sump and delivers it to the oil pump. There are many different Slant Six oil pans and matching pickup tubes, so it is a good idea to check the pickup to be sure it is centered in the pan's sump and close to the floor of the oil pan. An incorrect and/or mispositioned oil pickup tube will uncover and suck air during hard stops, fast acceleration, or aggressive cornering.*

3 *Clean and inspect the oil pan pickup tube, looking closely for possible cracks in the pipe thread that mounts the tube into the engine block. Screw the tube into the block and use the bare oil pan (no gaskets) to check the tube's position in the sump. Dab some grease on the edges of the pickup's screen enclosure to get a "fingerprint" mark on the oil pan floor. Adjust the tube's position by screwing and unscrewing it or by carefully bending it.*

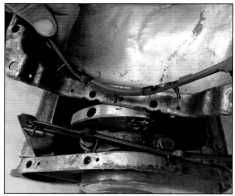

4 *The Slant Six uses a four-piece oil pan gasket consisting of two rubber end seals and two long side rail gaskets. The rubber end seals install by pulling rubber tabs through small holes in the sheet metal. To make tab installation easier, inspect the surfaces of the sheet metal, file away any sharp edges, and deburr the entry of the small tab mounting holes.*

5 *Place a small bead of sealer in the corners where the timing chain cover meets the oil pan rail. The oil pan's front rubber end seal fits into this corner snugly, so a small amount of sealer is all that is needed to ensure oil does not have a path out between the bottom of the timing chain cover gasket and the pan's end seal.*

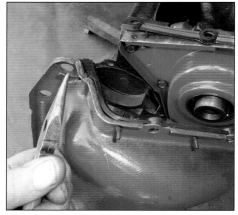

6 *Use needle-nose pliers to stretch and pull the tabs through the mounting holes. A small dab of grease or RTV sealer on the tabs and a rotating action as you stretch and pull on the tab will help slide it into place. For the best access, install the front oil pan end seal into the timing chain cover before installing the vibration damper.*

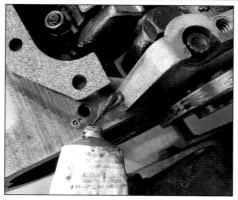

7 Now is a good time to check the oil pan and pickup tube clearance to the crankshaft. Set the pan in position without the pan's side rail gaskets, install a couple of finger-tight bolts, and then rotate the crank a few revolutions while listening for any interference. The key here is to make sure the crank's counterweights do not hit the oil pickup tube. Here is an oil pan ready-to-install checklist: bearing caps torqued, oil pickup tube installed, oil pan end seals installed, main seal tabs glued down, and nothing is hitting on the crankshaft.

8 The rear of the oil pan gasket has two places where three separate pieces come together to make the seal. The main seal cap L tabs form the base, and those are overlapped by the oil pan side rail gaskets. The oil pan's rear rubber end seal compresses the rail gasket onto the L tab to form a tight seal. When done correctly, this stack of materials seals well without the use of sealers, but we like to add a dab of RTV sealer in the corners just to be sure there is no pathway for oil to escape.

9 There are two more overlap joints at the front of the oil pan's rail gaskets. The front rubber end seal provides the base, and the side rail gaskets lie on top of the rubber blocks at the corners. There are two raised bumps on the rubber front seal corners to help position the rail gaskets. Place some sealer in these corners to plug any possible gaps.

10 Glue the oil pan side rail gasket to the block to hold everything in place while the oil pan is installed. This is what the rear junction looks like before the oil pan is set in place.

11 A view of the front rail gasket to end seal overlap joint with sealer. The oil pan is now ready to install.

12 Place the oil pan on the engine and start the two bolts at the rear that screw into the main seal cap. These two bolts are longer than all the others and thread into aluminum, so oil the bolt threads and be careful to avoid crossthreading. Start the bolts and give them a few turns then move to the front of the oil pan and start but do not tighten the four bolts that thread into the base of the timing chain cover.

Installing the Oil Pan CONTINUED

13 *With the front and rear oil pan bolts started, install the remaining side rail bolts. These bolts should start easily with your fingers. Get all the bolts started before drawing any one bolt down because this lets the oil pan "float" and align with the other bolt holes as you install all of the bolts. Once all the bolts are started, tighten down the oil pan from the center and outward to the ends to prevent the side rail gaskets from wrinkling. Draw the pan down evenly and tighten to 200 in-lbs.*

14 *The final oil pan gasket installation and tightening should draw the oil pan onto the gasket and displace some of the sealer, without over-compressing and crushing the gaskets. Make sure the cover or pan is making complete contact with the gasket(s) by looking for gaps along the gasket joint or loose bolt head washers, indicating that the bolt has jammed in its threads prior to compressing the cover and gasket. Stop tightening the cover bolts once you see contact.*

15 *It is better to under-tighten than do a retighten on the oil pan gasket. Overtightening the multielement oil pan gasket quickly overcompresses the side rail gaskets, bulging and splitting those gaskets at the bolt holes. Watch the gaskets closely as you tighten the bolts. Stop tightening once you see the material compressing but before it starts bulging out the sides of the oil pan.*

The valve cover should be left off until the engine is installed, started, and tuned, so we will not review its installation in this section.

Expansion and Pipe Plugs

Slant Six water jacket freeze plugs are cup-style expansion plugs with 1⅝-inch diameter. They are offered in a deep or shallow cup configuration. The factory used the shallow type, but the block will accept either plug depth without problems.

Freeze plugs are made in galvanized steel, brass, and stainless steel material. They are priced accordingly, so decide if the added cost justifies the increased corrosion resistance you get from brass or stainless. We have found that painting the entire surface of a galvanized steel plug and maintaining your cooling system provides long freeze plug life.

There are a few other NPT plugs in the engine block, and now is a good time to also install those plugs. This helps you avoid an unintended fluid spill during engine start-up. One other plug to check is the oil pan drain plug. Make sure the pan's drain plug is installed, and put a wrench on it to be sure the plug is tight prior to starting and test-driving the new engine.

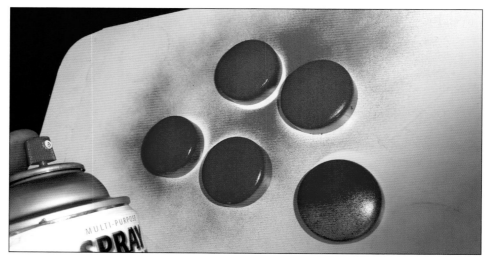

The Slant Six expansion plugs (freeze plugs) are 1⅝ inches in diameter and must be installed before the intake and exhaust manifold assembly. Deep or shallow wall plugs can be used. We like to etch and paint both sides of any galvanized steel replacement plugs to help prevent corrosion and future "rust-thru."

Use sandpaper or a round file to clean the walls of the freeze plug openings and wipe them clean. Use a sticky sealer in the hole and on the plug to make sure it stays in place when the cooling system is under pressure. Start the plug in the opening and drive it down evenly by using a flat piece of metal and a hammer. Once it is flush with the block, use a 1⅝-inch-diameter driver (a 1¼-inch socket works well) on the shoulder of the plug to drive it in a little farther.

Engine plugs include 1/8, 1/4, and 3/8 National Pipe Thread (NPT) plugs. These plugs can have a standard, raised square, or hex head and should be installed with some type of sealer on the threads. The common locations include the sending unit port on the oil pump and/or oil main gallery and the water jacket coolant drain plug. There are also plugs used in the intake manifold. Be sure to check the oil pan's drain plug to be sure it is installed and tight. Checking and installing these plugs now can avoid a big fluid cleanup later.

Cylinder Head Installation

The cylinder head gasket is the most important gasket in the engine. Care must be taken to install it correctly.

The coolant in a Slant Six flows from the water pump into the cylinder block then on to the rear of the engine. At the rear, the coolant flows up and through two large holes leading into the cylinder head. There are six smaller steam holes in the top deck and head gasket that are positioned right under each exhaust port; these holes direct colder block coolant up and directly around these hot running ports. The coolant flows forward through the head, out the thermostat cover outlet, and back into the top tank of the radiator.

To get this coolant flow path, the head gasket needs to seal off around these coolant passages and plug off a couple of other large sandcasting core holes in the block's top deck that lead into the cylinder head. Factory steel shim head gaskets can rust out at these core hole locations, and that allows coolant to take a shortcut from the front of the block straight up and right back out of the engine, without picking up any heat. Composite head gaskets seal the holes effectively, but steel shim gaskets may not keep them blocked over time, so it is best to plug these holes (or at least the front one) if you plan to use the embossed steel shim–type head gasket.

A good head gasket seal is dependent on clean, flat sealing surfaces. The head and the engine block's top deck should have been remachined to increase the engine's compression and to produce the clean and flat surfaces required for proper head gasket sealing.

Slant Six head gaskets come in a few different material types, constructions, coatings, and thicknesses. Review the head gasket you have to see if it is a good match for your new engine. In general, the embossed steel shim–style head gasket is the thinnest, and it is what the factory used on many Slant Six engines. This gasket has a compressed thickness of 0.020 inch, and it needs freshly machined surfaces and some spray sealer to achieve a good seal.

When using an embossed steel shim head gasket, tap and install a pipe plug into the forward top deck sandcasting hole. This prevents gasket rust-out and a coolant flow short-circuit that can erroneously drop the out-going coolant temperature at the thermostat and temperature sending unit location.

The embossed steel shim head gasket does not come in aftermarket gasket kits, so you will have to find and purchase one separately. A composite material head gasket will come in today's gasket kits, and those gaskets vary in construction and thickness, depending on the manufacturer. A good-quality aftermarket composite head gasket for the Slant Six is the Fel-Pro Printoseal unit that has a compressed thickness of 0.040 inch and comes with a coating and additional sealing materials already applied. Other manufacturer's composite gaskets are thicker (up to 0.055 inch compressed) and come with and without topical coatings.

A composite gasket is more "forgiving" and seals well on surfaces that are not freshly machined, but it is a thicker gasket and will drop the compression ratio by about 1/3 of a point (0.3) when directly replacing an embossed steel shim head gasket (with no head or block deck resurfacing work). Solid copper head gaskets are also available in different thicknesses for the engine, but this type of gasket takes extra effort to effectively seal, so it should only be used for high-performance and racing applications.

There are a few preparation steps and related parts that need to be installed before bolting the head onto the engine. The most important thing is to get all of the camshaft lifters installed before placing the head gasket and cylinder head onto the short-block assembly. This is especially important with the 1975–1980 no spark plug tube heads because the lifters cannot be accessed once the cylinder head is installed.

Installing the Cylinder Head

1 Slant Six lifters are 0.904-inch diameter, which is the same as many of the Chrysler V-8 engines. There are different solid lifter styles: straight sided or barbell shaped. Most of the factory-installed solid lifters are the barbell style, which can be lighter and hold additional oil in the center gap. Aftermarket replacement lifters are usually straight sided and the weight (and quality) varies. Solid lifters can be resurfaced and reused, so call around to machine shops and camshaft grinders about that option.

2 Install the lifters before installing the cylinder head. This is especially important with non–spark plug tube cylinder heads because there is no lifter bore access once the head is installed. Use a high-pressure lubricant on the lifter face and standard engine assembly lube on the lifter's side and in the bore. The lifters should slide smoothly into the bores, so do additional deburring or cleaning if they feel tight or rough.

Installing the Cylinder Head CONTINUED

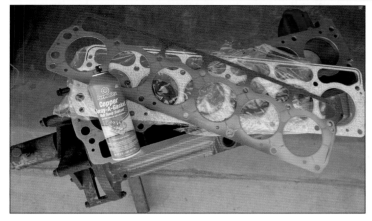

3 There are a few different types of Slant Six cylinder head gaskets; the factory primarily used a stamped and embossed steel gasket that measures 0.020 inch thick. Aftermarket head gaskets are constructed from a composite of materials and range in thickness from 0.040 to 0.060 inch. Be sure to measure the gasket you have and use its thickness when doing your compression ratio calculation. Some aftermarket gaskets already have a sticky coating applied to them, but others are dry. We spray the uncoated ones with a sealer prior to installation.

4 A common leak point on a Slant Six is along the lifter pocket on the passenger's side of the engine. This aftermarket head gasket already had a bead of sealer along this edge, but only on one side. We added sealer on the other side to reduce the chance of oil getting through. Also make sure the surface around the top of each cylinder bore is clean and damage free because this is where the "fire ring" of the head gasket will make its seal.

5 Position the head gasket on the engine's top deck locating dowel pins and set the cylinder head onto the engine. We bolt a bare rocker arm shaft to the head to serve as an easy-to-grip handle to help lift the head into position, but you can easily make a handle by drilling a couple of holes through a piece of 1/2-inch PVC pipe or electrical conduit.

6 Apply some moly lube around each head bolt hole opening and to the threads of each bolt. Start the bolts by hand to be sure they thread in smoothly, and then draw them down snug with your favorite wrench.

7 Torque the cylinder head bolts to 80 ft-lbs by starting in the center and working outward, in a crisscross pattern. If torquing the bolts in stages, always have more torque on the center bolts and spread the clamping force out to the ends to prevent wrinkling the gasket.

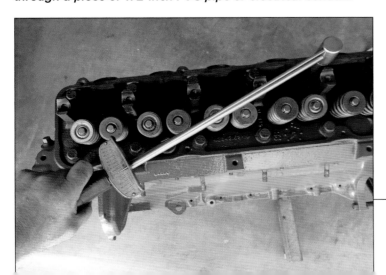

Rocker Arm Assembly

The Slant Six rocker arm may look funny, but it is an engineering marvel. The arm is stamped, embossed, folded, coined, assembled, threaded, and heat treated to produce a strong and lightweight assembly.

Early rocker arms had the rocker shaft sleeve pressed-in and welded to the main rocker arm body, while later units were staked together at the rocker shaft tube. The welding was inconsistent and known to crack, and the small embossed oil passages inside the rocker arm get clogged, so be sure to inspect and

replace any defective units you find.

It is important to get the pushrods and rocker arm assembly parts in place once the lifters and cylinder head are installed. This way, the lifters are captured and will not fall out of their bores if you turn the engine assembly over on the engine stand. Don't ask us how we know this . . .

Installing the Pushrods

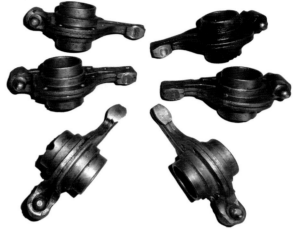

1 Early rocker arms had the rocker shaft sleeve welded to the main rocker arm body, while later units were staked. Inspect the rocker arms to be sure the sleeve is secure, especially with the welded version. Weld quality varied and the sleeve can break free at the weld, rotate in the arm, and plug off the rocker arm's oil feed passages.

2 Inspect the rocker arm tips for wear and damage. Light wear will show as a shiny spot that should be centered on the tip's contact pad. Moderate wear or rust pitting will produce an uneven surface that you can feel, indicating that the pad needs to be resurfaced. The rocker arm should be replaced if you find heavy wear or damage to the tip's pad.

3 There were two different rocker arm shafts used during production. The early shaft had 7/16-inch-diameter bolt holes and a notch or "flat" on the top front edge of the shaft to indicate correct installation orientation. Later shafts had one smaller mounting bolt hole at the bottom rear of the shaft and used a special shoulder bolt with a smaller 5/16-18 thread to make sure the shaft (and its oil feed holes) were in the correct position. All the shafts use 5/8 expansion plugs in the shaft's ends that can be removed by punching sideways and then pulling them out with pliers.

Installing the Pushrods CONTINUED

4 We have tried many different cleaning methods on Slant Six rocker arm assemblies and found that caustic soda or baking in a high-temperature oven tend to clog up the small oil passages in the rocker arms. Solvent cleaning, with good old-fashioned elbow grease, gives us the best results. We send really greasy assemblies through the Jet-Washer first and then solvent clean afterward. The rocker shaft is just over 26 inches long, so we made a 28-inch-long cleaning pan out of some rain gutter material to minimize the amount of solvent needed. Small pieces of rubber hose are used on the bolt threads to keep the bolts and their spaces with the assembly.

5 Use a can of spray carburetor cleaner with the nozzle tube to flush out all of the small oil passages in the rocker arms. Insert the tube into the oil port exit on the top of the arm (pushrod and lifter oiling hole) and give the arm a shot of spray. The cleaner will come out of the tip opening (valve stem oiling hole) if all the oil passages are clear and flowing.

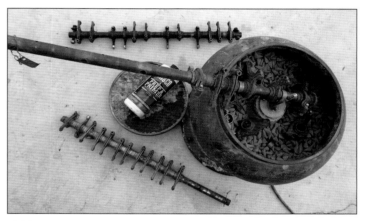

6 Rusty rocker arms present another cleaning challenge. Most machine shops will take the time to bead blast each arm then solvent clean them again. This works okay, but we prefer to use a vibratory tumbler and some rust remover solution to get rusty rocker arms shiny again. Most precision machine shops have this type of deburring equipment, so ask around to see if someone can do this type of cleaning for you.

7 Used pushrods can be cleaned and checked for straightness by rolling them on a hard, flat surface, such as a tabletop or a car hood or trunk lid. Clean the cup end of each pushrod for painting and then line them all up, close together, for a quick spot of contrasting paint color. The goal is to end up with a visible paint dab on one side of the rod, near the cup. This paint mark will make it easy to see if all the pushrods (and the lifters below) are spinning, once the engine is started.

Installing the Pushrods CONTINUED

8 Drop each pushrod into position with the cup side facing up, and check to be sure the ball end seats into the lifter socket. (Hydraulic lifter Slant Six pushrods are symmetrical, so install either way.) We wrap a piece of sandpaper around a piece of 3/4-inch wooden dowel and clean off the rocker arm shaft "saddles" on the top of each head tower, just to be sure they are clean and undamaged.

9 Inspect the sanded rocker arm mounting saddles to be sure they are clean and smooth. This rear tower saddle had a couple of nicks, but they did not have raised edges and did not extend into the pressurized oil pathway. This rocker arm assembly is okay to install. The rocker arm shaft should seal tightly against all the saddles to prevent oil from escaping at those joints instead of flowing into each rocker arm.

10 Set the rocker arm assembly onto the cylinder head saddles and place all the retaining bolts and spacers into the shaft holes, then thread the bolts in a couple of turns. Move the rocker arms side to side to be sure none of their edges are trapped on top of a mounting tower saddle. Find the tallest pushrods and make sure their rocker arm adjuster ball-screw is sitting in the pushrod's cup before tightening down the assembly.

11 The rocker arm shaft assembly goes together as follows: the shaft has the index notch facing forward and up (oil feed holes face the valves and point downward), the end bolt with short-tabbed washer, rocker arm, ring spacer, rocker arm, bolt with short-tabbed washer, rocker arm, ring spacer, rocker arm. Repeat until you reach the center shaft bolt hole, where the only wide-tabbed washer in the set is used.

12 All of the rocker arms, shaft spacers, short-tabbed washers, and short bolts are the same and can be used in any position. The exceptions are the wider-tabbed washer that is used at the center of the shaft and the longer mounting bolt that is used at the rear of the assembly. Oil flows up through the rear shaft mounting tower, around the longer bolt's shank, and into the shaft on its way out to each rocker arm. The tabbed washers will often have different tab sizes, so selectively fit them into places that help position the rocker arm's pad directly over each valve stem tip.

13 Loosen each rocker arm adjusting ball-screw a turn or two so they are all too loose, then evenly tighten down the rocker shaft assembly. Inspect all of the rocker arm pad to valve stem contact positions and reposition any tabbed washers, if needed. Once everything is correctly positioned, torque the rocker arm shaft retaining bolts to 30 ft-lbs and do a cold valve lash clearance adjustment using the ICEO method described earlier.

Intake and Exhaust Manifold Installation

The production Slant Six intake and exhaust manifold set is an assembly made up of two separate manifolds. The manifolds are bolted together in a way that provides exhaust gas heating onto the bottom of the induction manifold. The intake manifold for a 1-barrel carburetor is the most common one found, but the factory did offer 2- and 4-barrel manifolds over the years.

The intake manifolds were made in cast iron, cast aluminum, and even a lightweight two-piece die-cast aluminum assembly that was e-beam welded together. The aftermarket produced and still produces many different Slant Six intake manifolds, tube steel headers, and replacement exhaust manifolds, which we will review in a different section of this book. All of these manifolds install onto the engine in the same basic way, with heat expansion of the exhaust manifold being the biggest area of concern and failures.

The factory cast-iron "six-into-one" exhaust manifold is long and needs room to expand and contract as it goes through heat cycles. The factory used special fasteners and a specific torque to allow for some movement. Using the wrong fasteners and/or incorrect manifold set installation will result in leaks, broken studs, or a warped, cracked, or broken exhaust manifold. This is a frequent problem area with the Slant Six, so proper manifold inspection, preparation, and correct installation is extremely important. Last reminder: install the freeze plugs before installing the manifold assembly.

Installing the Intake and Exhaust Manifold

1 Use a manifold gasket or a straight-edge to check the port opening alignment on the intake and exhaust manifold set. Slant Six exhaust manifolds can warp, bend, and crack, especially if the wrong fasteners are installed or if the manifolds are not tightened correctly. Broken end studs are a sign that the exhaust manifold may be warped.

Installing the Intake and Exhaust Manifold *CONTINUED*

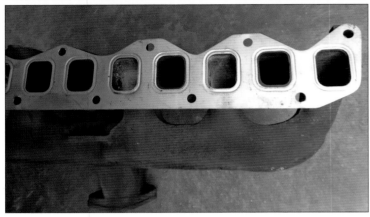

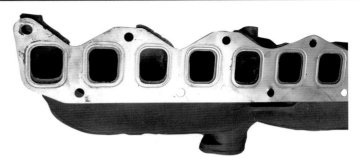

2 *Using the manifold gasket as a template, we see that the intake and exhaust ports are well aligned at the front of this manifold assembly.*

3 *The port alignment was not as good at the rear of the manifold set. The exhaust ports move higher in relation to the intake ports, with the end exhaust port about 3/16 inch higher than the neighboring intake opening. This was likely caused by a broken manifold mounting stud in the top rear location.*

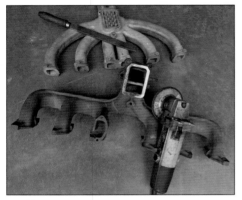

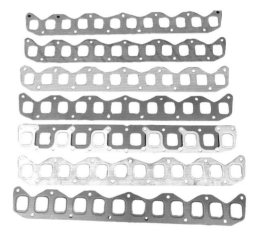

4 *Slight port misalignment can be adjusted out by grinding or filing material off the corresponding edges of the heat riser valve gasket sealing surfaces. This only works if one end is high and the other is low. Replace the exhaust manifold if both end ports have drifted higher than the intake ports next to it.*

5 *The manifold assembly should be resurfaced if it has been taken apart and reassembled. Spend time carefully aligning the two manifolds so all the ports are level prior to resurfacing. You may need to drill out the heat box attachment bolt holes in the intake manifold or do some other grinding to get the clearance needed for good manifold-to-manifold alignment.*

6 *Intake and exhaust manifold gaskets come in a number of types. The factory used an embossed steel shim gasket, but a steel core composite gasket often comes in today's aftermarket gasket sets. As with the steel shim head gasket, the embossed steel shim manifold gasket should only be used if the head's port surface and manifolds have been remachined and are completely flat.*

7 *Thick paper and high-temperature graphite material gaskets, such as the Remflex 6008, are also available. They work well if the manifold or the cylinder head's gasket surface has not been resurfaced. The manifold set moves around on the head as it heats and cools, so the graphite material helps it slide around during temperature cycling.*

8 The manifold gasket is a great template to check port alignment and correct manifold placement. Lay the gasket onto the head and then onto the manifold set to check the relationship between the ports and gasket. The gasket openings should match or be slightly larger than the ports, and the gasket edges should never overhang into the ports. We center the gasket on the manifold assembly's face and then paint or scribe marks onto the gasket to give us a visual reference for the correct positioning of the parts when they are installed.

9 It is a good idea to do a test fit of the manifold assembly onto the head studs before installing the gasket or lubricating the mounting stud threads. Make sure the manifolds slide onto the studs easily and that there is some clearance around all the studs so the assembly can float as it heats and cools. Apply high-temp anti-seize compound to all of the stud threads to make installation and future fastener removal easier.

10 The manifold's port openings should be as high as possible in relation to the head ports to help improve airflow and fuel suspension. Enlarge and grind around the manifold set's mounting studs and through holes to get additional movement. Let gravity help by installing the manifold assembly with the engine up side down on the stand. This orientation also gives more access to the hard-to-reach lower manifold mounting studs.

11 The manifold hardware is designed to let the manifolds expand and contract while keeping them firmly pressed to the gasket. The 1/2-inch hex steel retaining nuts have a 5/16-24 UNF thread, but the two nuts used on the end studs are special locking nuts. There are three different washers used. One is a cast-iron cup washer used at the center top intake manifold through hole. Spanner washers are used on 10 studs that clamp the intake and exhaust manifolds at the same time. Two brass washers are used on the end exhaust manifold through holes with the special slotted locking nuts. Later engines used a thicker spanner washer that is more resistant to bending.

12 With the manifold assembly in position, use two screwdrivers to get the spanner washers onto the studs. The bottom studs in the center are hard to reach, so slide a washer onto a long rod or Phillips screwdriver, touch it to the end of the stud, and then slide the washer onto the stud with another screwdriver. The nuts can be started using a socket and extension, but you may have to place two nuts into the socket so one stays out at the end, where you can see it.

13 The special slotted acorn nuts go on each end stud with the slotted end fitting into the large countersink on the brass washer. Be sure the spanner washers have clearance around their sides, especially where they meet the exhaust manifold. Do not let the spanner washers rotate as you tighten them because that may jam the washer into the manifold and limit expansion movement. Torque the nuts to 15 ft-lbs maximum.

Water, Fuel, and Oil Pump

Install the water, fuel, and oil pumps onto the long-block assembly while the engine is still on the engine stand. The pumps used on the Slant Six are all available new, so it is best to purchase and replace these items instead of reusing or rebuilding them. The only exception to this rule is the oil pump, which tends to be more expensive and have questionable drive gear quality.

Installing these parts is easy. Be sure to use the correct fasteners and some sealer to prevent leaks. A part identification review, some preinstall checks, and a few installation tips are needed to be successful with this phase of engine assembly.

Chrysler engineers paid attention to every little detail, and that discipline carried over to the water pump. Early road tests found that the pump shaft's drain hole could get plugged with road dirt and grime, so a protective shield was added to the housing to prevent this problem. The different-length 170 versus 225 (G versus RG) coolant bypass hose length is also apparent.

Water pumps for the Slant Six come in a variety of materials and impeller types. Early pumps were made out of cast iron and have a 3.5-inch-round impeller that was also cast iron. Later water pump housings were die-cast aluminum and fitted with either the round cast-iron or a stamped-steel paddle–type impeller. The die-cast pump housing required a separate divider plate, captured between the low-pressure suction side and the higher-pressure water jacket sides of the pump. As a result, two water pump to block sealing gaskets are needed to successfully install the die-cast water pump. Stamped-steel pump impellers are found with six and eight blades. The current eight-blade pumps have a funnel-shaped divider plate that helps reduce cavitation around the impeller blades.

Cut a viewing window into an old water pump to check the pump's impeller clearance and the critical pinch point (where the coolant is pushed into the block's water jacket). The pump develops the most pressure and flow when the impeller is close to the floor of the water pump scroll opening and its blades just miss the protruding side wall, where the entry to the block's water jacket is located. The gap between the impeller and the side wall can be adjusted by drilling or reaming the pump's mounting holes oversize and pushing the pump closer to the wall, then marking the position.

Installing the Water Pump

1 Some water pump housings have a large step where the inlet meets the impeller cavity. Use a ball burr or a round file to remove this raised edge and promote smoother coolant flow through the water pump.

2 Line up the divider plate with the two gaskets. Use some sealer on both sides of the gaskets and on the threads of the lower through hole bolt to help prevent water leaks.

3 Install the coolant bypass hose with its two clamps positioned as shown, then mount the water pump with the correct-length bolts. The two longer bolts install next to the inlet opening and have a 1¾ inch underhead length. One of these bolts fits into a blind hole, and the other goes through into the water jacket in front of the first cylinder barrel. As a result, longer replacement bolts may bottom out before drawing the water pump tightly against the mounting surfaces.

Installing the Fuel Pump

1 Slant Six fuel pumps are offered as a seal unit or a bolt-together assembly that is rebuildable. Both types interchange and install in the same way, but the bolt-together type has a threaded outlet fitting, allows for different port clocking, and can be modified internally, if needed.

2 To most mechanics, the Slant Six fuel pump appears to be mounted upside down, but the ports-up orientation is correct. Pump installation is easy when the pump's accentuation arm is on the low side of the camshaft's driving eccentric lobe. Rotate the engine a little if the pump does not easily line up with its mounting holes. The mounting holes are "blind," so sealing the threads is not required as long as you use the correct-length fasteners. We like to stick the gasket to the block with sealer and leave the pump side dry.

Installing the Oil Pump

1 Slant Six oil pump drive gear failure has been a problem, so we do everything possible to prevent it. The gear that comes on a replacement aftermarket oil pump is unproven. We prefer to reuse an OEM gear that shows a good wear pattern and has a known history. A tie-rod end puller is used here to remove the gear from a factory pump. Pump gears without a keyway can also be removed by taking the impeller cover off the pump and then pressing the impeller shaft out of the gear. Heat the gear and freeze the pump shaft to make gear reinstallation easier.

2 Oil pump gaskets from different suppliers have slightly different designs around the oil pickup to pump port, and some gaskets do not fully seal. Check this by fitting the gasket to the engine block and to the oil pump to be sure there are no gaps or thin sealing overlap areas where oil can leak out and air gets sucked into the system. We cut, fit, and glue in an extra piece of gasket material in this location to make sure no leaks occur.

3 Attach the oil pump's gasket to the block and put a small amount of Vaseline into the impeller cavity of the pump to help it develop suction upon start-up. Lubricate the pump's drive gear with moly lube and install the oil pump.

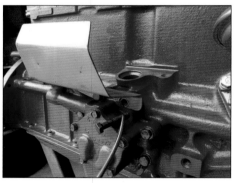

Many Slant Six engines were equipped with a splash shield that helped protect the distributor from water and water mist. This part is often bent, broken, or missing. It is not essential, especially in dry areas or on vehicles that are primarily driven in nice weather. Use the shield if you plan to drive in rainy conditions or off-road. The shield is held on by the top two oil pump mounting bolts, and it acts as the washers for those two bolts.

Damper, Brackets, and Mounts

The vibration damper can be installed once the timing chain cover and oil pan are in place. Lubricate the front seal and use a damper installation tool or a bolt with a stack of large washers to draw the damper onto the snout of the crankshaft. Do not pound the damper onto the crank with a hammer; doing so can damage the damper and/or the crankshaft thrust bearing.

There are a few other brackets and the engine mounts (motor mounts) that should be installed now, before lifting the engine off the stand and placing it into the vehicle.

The vibration damper is best installed by using a special tool that threads into the front of the crankshaft and has a separate nut that pushes the damper onto the crankshaft snout. A large bolt with flat washers can also be used, but never attempt to install the damper by pounding it on with a hammer.

Paint the timing marks with white paint so they stand out clearly when viewed with a timing light. We add additional marks at 25, 30, and 35 degrees advance because this helps set the total timing. Use the factory timing tab and damper's top dead center (TDC) mark to find 10 degrees advance, then reference that new mark to find 25 and 30 degrees advanced. The 30 degree advance mark should be 1⅞ inches away from the TDC mark in the clockwise direction.

Cast-iron and stamped-steel alternator mounting brackets were used over the years. Most placed the alternator and the coil on the passenger's side of the engine. Early vehicles and some vans had a driver-side steel bracket without coil mounting. Inspect the bracket for cracks and rounded-out holes, especially the stamped-steel version.

Passenger-side alternator brackets have three mounting bolt holes: two go into the block and one into the head. The rearmost hole uses a smaller 5/16-18 UNC bolt and the two forward holes have 3/8-16 UNC threads. The forward, upper head casting hole is "blind," but the lower one is a through hole leading into the block's pushrod area.

Use some thread sealer on the front lower alternator bracket mounting bolt to keep oil from seeping out through the threads. We forgot to do this ahead of time, so we pulled out and sealed this bolt after the engine was installed.

Install the driver-side engine mount assembly (bracket and cushion) and the engine to transmission bellhousing support bracket. Both of these brackets use 7/16-14-UNC bolts (5/8 hex-head). Leave the bolts a turn loose so the brackets can be shifted around as you align and install other bolts that fasten them down.

The passenger-side motor mount and bracket tucks up under the fuel pump. It is attached to the block with two 7/16-14 UNC hex-head bolts. Position the assembly with the mount cushion at the top and the steel bracket pointing down, as shown.

Hybrid Slant Six Engine Combinations

We have built a lot of special Slant Six engines over the years. Many of these engines combine factory parts in different configurations to enhance performance. Modern metric pistons in the 87.5- to 89-mm range are the key change that many of these special engines share. These pistons are lighter, use thinner rings, and have a shorter compression height, which all benefit performance.

Here is an overview of three of these hybrid combinations, highlighting the parts used, special machine work (if needed), and the performance difference the combination created.

Many performance Slant Six engine buildups are based on using the 7-inch-long center-to-center 198 connecting rod and a lightweight 2.2 piston that has thin ring packs. The aftermarket supports this approach with custom-made 7-inch center-to-center H-beam rods and special forged pistons. This combination of parts produces high compression ratios without cylinder head and block deck milling, so race gas or fuel additives may be needed to successfully run a "long rod" Slant Six engine.

Extra care goes into building a high-performance race engine, as shown here with the bottom end of a 7-inch rod plus stroked crankshaft Slant Six. The connecting rods are made of chrome-moly steel and the crankshaft has been fully deburred, polished, and nitrided.

Long Rod "RG" 225

This combination uses the longer 198 Slant Six connecting rod and 2.2 Chrysler 4-cylinder piston combined with a 225 block and crankshaft. The 198 connecting rod is 7.006 inches long, and the lighter 2.2 piston has a 1.6-inch compression height, thinner rings, and the same piston pin size as the Slant Six (0.901). Standard 2.2 bore size is 87.5 mm (3.445), so this is basically a 0.045 oversize piston.

This is a bolt-together combination that produces a higher compression ratio with a lighter piston, less ring friction, and improved connecting rod ratio. The 198 Slant Six engines were only produced for five years, so finding the 7-inch connecting rods is difficult. There is a wide selec-

tion of 2.2 pistons with different piston head dishes and valve reliefs, but compression ratios start out in the mid 9:1 area and go up into 11:1 zone without block or cylinder head milling. This combination makes a "free-spinning," high-compression 225, so it is best built as a performance engine that can rev up into the higher RPM.

Low-Block "G" 198

The smaller and lighter 170 low-deck G Slant Six engine block and its 5.7-inch center-to-center connecting rods are combined with the 198 Slant Six crankshaft to make a 170 with an increased stroke and higher compression. Up to 210 ci can be achieved (3.640 stroke x 89 mm bore) in the smaller and lighter 170 engine block. This engine has a near "square" bore to stroke relationship and is comfortable running in the higher RPM ranges.

The shorter, lighter, less-drag 2.2 pistons are used to help the engine rev and to get the compression ration into a reasonable range. Once again, finding a 198 crankshaft is difficult. The first and last crankshaft counterweights interfere with the bottoms of the number-1 and number-6 pistons. Minor crankshaft counterweight reduction grinding and crank rebalancing is needed to get the larger crank to clear the piston bottoms, but everything else fits together well. The only real advantage to the combination is its smaller size and lower weight compared to a standard "RG" 198.

Stroked Crankshaft 260 "RG"

Welding up the crankshaft's connecting rod journals and offset grinding the rod throws to increase the engine's stroke is the main focus of this special engine combination. The stroke on a 225 Slant Six is 4.125 inches, but it is possible to increase the stroke by 3/8 inch to 4.5 inches. The 4.5-inch stroke combined with a 3.504-inch bore (0.104 oversize bore at 89 mm) yields a 260.36-ci Slant Six engine.

The 4.5-inch stroke still uses the 6.7-inch center-to-center 225 connecting rod. The added crank stroke requires some connecting rod clearance notch grinding at the bottom of the cylinder bores and connecting rod cap clearancing along the driver-side wall of the engine block. With this work, the longer stroke can be made to fit into the engine. We did a second "5/16" (4.440) stroked 225 crankshaft, and that stroke length fit into the engine block with very little grinding work. It is the stroke increase we recommend for an RG Slant Six engine block.

Hybrid Slant Six Engine Combinations *CONTINUED*

Turbo 2.2 Chrysler 4-cylinder pistons with a 16-cc dish or Chrysler 2.5 pistons are needed to keep the compression ratio reasonable for pump gas. The big problem with this combination is finding a shop that will weld up and offset grind a Slant Six crankshaft at an affordable cost. The resulting "big inch" Slant Six is powerful and has increased torque, but the extra-long stroke does not lend itself to higher RPM. ■

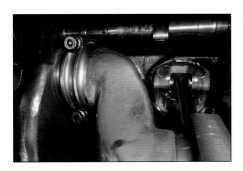

A closer look at this stroker engine shows the forged pistons and hard-faced camshaft lobes. The engine fasteners are aftermarket replacements made of high-strength materials. All of the parts used in the rotating assembly have been rebalanced.

The fun thing with a long rod Slant Six is that it can be made to look like any other Slant . . . but it runs better.

Aluminum Block

The die-cast aluminum Slant Six cylinder block was produced in low volume. This version of the Slant Six has a number of significant differences when compared to the cast-iron block engines. The aluminum Slant Six engine size, shape, and installation are the same as all other RG Slant Sixes, but, in truth, it is a very different engine.

The aluminum engine is fragile and harder to assemble. It is not forgiving when it comes to maintenance, overheating, or general driving abuse. It is best used as a show engine rather than a daily driver or a performance engine. Water jacket corrosion is the biggest problem we see with this engine, followed by head gasket failure.

The unique features of the aluminum engine are mostly internal. Those items will be reviewed here so you can correctly identify that version of the Slant Six or its special parts when you see them. We do not have space in this book to cover all of the specialized assembly information needed to rebuild the aluminum Slant Six, so refer to the Factory Service Manual for that information.

The aluminum-block Slant Six special parts:

- Die-cast aluminum cylinder block
- Main bearing caps and bolts
- Upper rear main seal cap, bolts, and seal
- Cylinder head and bolts
- Head gasket
- Oil gallery plugs ■

Many aluminum-block Slant Six engines are painted or greasy, so it is hard to tell that the block is made of aluminum. The driver's side of the aluminum block is somewhat smooth and does not have any freeze plugs.

The passenger's side of the block has deep recesses around each cylinder bore and three thin ribs that extend out to the back of the timing chain's cover flange. A magnet will not stick to any of the external engine block surfaces.

A closer look at the engine shows the open top deck surface and the integrally casted-in cylinder liners. The special cylinder head gasket seals on the thin edge of the cast-iron liners. The engine ID stamping tells us that this core is a 1962 aluminum engine assembled on November 30 (SA 1130) and that the top deck surface has never been resurfaced.

Aluminum Block CONTINUED

This is the 35,999 aluminum block cast, as shown by the number stamped into the passenger's side of the rear mounting flange. The bosses along the oil gallery were designed to be drilled and provide pressurized oil to the lifter bores so hydraulic lifters could be used. Production engines never used this feature, and some aluminum blocks do not have these bosses.

The rear of this engine shows a previous weld repair and new pinholes around the weld where coolant was leaking. This is a common corrosion location on these blocks. The camshaft expansion plug shown is 1.976, which is different from the cast-iron block's plug. The rear oil gallery plug is also a larger size and is sealed with an O-ring.

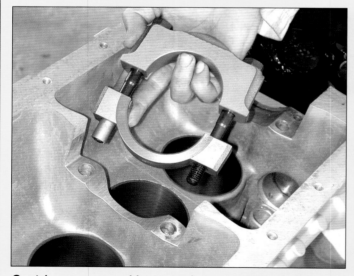

Cast-iron upper and lower main caps were used to provide more thermo-expansion stability for the main bearings. These caps require longer main cap bolts with a recess above the threads to allow oil to pass from the block into the upper cap and out to the crankshaft bearing. There are locating sleeves used to help position the upper caps into recesses in block. (Photo Courtesy Steve Magnante)

It is exciting to find an aluminum Slant Six engine block, but it is not worth much if it is missing its upper and lower main bearing caps and special bolts. ARP can make the special fasteners, and the lower caps are the same as the cast-iron engine, but the upper main caps are unique and extremely difficult to find.

The rear main seal uses the same upper and lower cap design with longer fasteners, as seen with the main bearings. The lower seal cap is the same as the cast-iron engine, but the upper cap is an "aluminum engine only" part. The good news is that a common lower cap can be machined into the aluminum engine's special upper cap and the longer 5/16-18 UNC fasteners are available as socket cap bolts. (Photo Courtesy Steve Magnante)

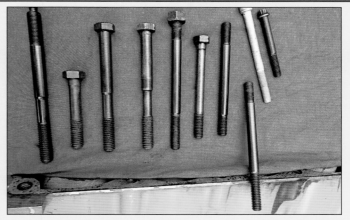

Aluminum-block head bolts have longer threads that are needed to spread the torque load over more area. From left to right: ARP replacement aluminum-block main stud with windage tray mounting, cast-iron block main bolt, aluminum-block main bolt with thick recess, aluminum-block main bolt with thin recess, ARP aluminum-block head stud with longer threads, cast-iron block head bolt, ARP cast-iron block head stud, ARP aluminum-block stud placed near its threaded deck hole boss, aluminum-block rear main seal cap bolt, and a cast-iron main seal cap bolt.

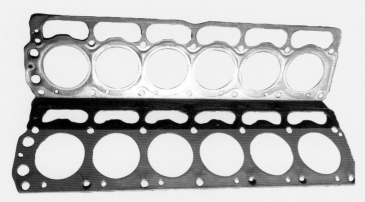

The head gasket used on the aluminum-block Slant Six has a different shape. The cast-iron engine's head gasket will not cover the open deck area found on the aluminum block. The heads used on the aluminum engine were "high accuracy" and had a star or the word "SPECIAL" cast into them. Other tube-type Slant Six heads can be used if carefully aligned over the cylinders. Later "no spark plug tube" Slant Six cylinder heads cannot be used on the aluminum block because their shape does not completely cover the aluminum block's top deck.

The special aluminum engine head gasket is easy to identify because it has a layer of copper that seals against the open water jacket on the block side. This copper layer is folded over onto the head side to create the fire ring that seals each cylinder. There is a thick layer of varnish around the pushrod openings to help seal that area. This special head gasket is no longer produced, so contact an antique gasket supplier if you need one.

ENGINE INSTALLATION AND START-UP

We try to follow up on information about any new parts related to the Slant Six, and we are happy to report that the aftermarket continues to make new items for the engine. Two suppliers with new Slant Six products are TorqStorm Superchargers, providing supercharger kits, and Aussiespeed, providing intake manifolds and exhaust headers. We contacted both suppliers, and they provided their latest Slant Six products for us to review and test.

We decided to "shift gears" and use the factory specification rebuilt Slant Six we assembled in the previous chapters to test some of these new products. Our goal is to see how much additional performance we can get by using bolt-on parts on a basically stock but carefully rebuilt 225 engine. The following engine installation and testing work is going to diverge from our daily driver focus because we are installing this engine and the associated performance parts into my 1962 Dodge Lancer test mule vehicle. This is a 2,800-pound "drag car" with low rear axle gearing and soft suspension. Its purpose in life is to make wide-open-throttle quarter-mile passes as fast as possible. This is not a pretty car, but it is easy to work on, has a strong 904 transmission, has a 8¾ rear end, and passes tech inspection at the local drag strip.

Follow along as we install a stock Slant Six, fire it up, then add some special parts to see how fast we can make it go. Thanks again to TorqStorm and Aussiespeed for letting us test their products.

TorqStorm Kit Contents

It is always great when boxes of performance parts show up on the doorstep. We quickly unpacked our TorqStorm Supercharger kit, pulled out the installation instructions, and reviewed all the parts. We decided to install the bottom pulley and supercharger's mounting brackets to the engine before installing it in the vehicle. Our plan is to start the rebuilt engine without the blower, test and tune it, and then add the rest of the supercharger parts once the engine is in the car and running well.

TorqStorm's kit comes with all of the needed parts and a set of installation instructions. Our kit contained two extra pulleys and a second belt so we could test higher boost levels by changing pulley ratios.

The TorqStorm Supercharger kit for the Slant Six uses a centrifugal blower that is belt driven and "blows through" the carburetor. A 4-barrel carburetor and intake manifold is needed, so we decided to use the Aussiespeed short runner intake because it was what TorqStorm used when it developed the kit.

Engine Stand Assemblies

1 The supercharger's mounting bracket and the crankshaft pulley were installed on the engine before lifting the entire assembly into the engine compartment. This was done to have better access to align the main supercharger bracket and bracket spacer to the water pump mounting holes. Installing these parts now made tightening the bracket and pulley fasteners easy, but these parts could have been installed after the engine was in the car.

2 The belt tensioner was already mounted to the main bracket when we received the kit, and the longer mounting fasteners were also supplied. The stock water pump pulley is still used, but it has to be installed after the TorqStorm bracket assembly is mounted and torqued down to 30 ft-lbs.

3 The selected 4-barrel intake manifold was test fitted to the engine, and it needed a little clearance grinding around the mounting studs. This allowed the "butterfly" washers and nuts to slide on easily. We also drilled and tapped two additional manifold runner bosses with 1/8 NPT threads to provide extra vacuum pressure ports. Our setup will need pressure signals to the blow-off valve, vacuum/boost gauge, fuel pump, and pressure regulator, so having extra port locations is helpful.

4 The side wall under the carburetor mounting bolts is thick, so we drilled and tapped two 5/16-18 UNC linkage and return spring bracket mounting holes. Drill the holes blind and use a bottoming tap so these new holes do not break into the plenum area for possible leak points.

Flex Plate, Clutch, and Final Parts

The flex plate or flywheel and clutch parts can only be installed once the engine is off the engine stand, so have those parts staged and ready to go before you start hoisting it off the stand. Remember this important step because flex plate installation can get overlooked during the excitement and busyness of getting the engine off the stand and installed in the car. It is a lot of work to have to pull the engine back out of the vehicle because the flex plate did not get installed onto the back of the crankshaft (don't ask us how we know).

Off the Stand Assemblies

1 *The flex plate connects the engine to an automatic transmission's torque converter. Manual transmission–equipped vehicles will use a flywheel and clutch assembly (instead of a flex plate) to make this connection. Either setup will have to be installed once the engine is off the engine stand.*

2 *Chrysler flex plates come in different sizes, bolt patterns, and center hub diameters, so check to be sure the flex plate you have matches the crankshaft. Our Lancer has an aftermarket torque converter with larger mounting bolts, so the outer flex plate to converter mounting holes had to be drilled out. This bolt pattern only aligns one way, so mark the flex plate and the torque converter to avoid confusion about how the parts go together. The small hole in the flex plate, near the crankshaft mounting holes, is opposite from the drain plug in the converter.*

3 *The flex plate to crankshaft mounting bolts are special low-head high-strength bolts with a specific underhead length (UHL). Carefully check any nonfactory replacement bolt for correct fit. Torque these bolts to 55 ft-lbs with an impact wrench or hold the crankshaft from turning with a bolt in the front damper when torquing these bolts with a standard torque wrench.*

Off the Stand Assemblies *CONTINUED*

4 *There are two 3/8–16 UNC bolt holes on the top of the Slant Six cylinder head that are used to lift the engine or engine and transmission assembly. Use a smooth strap fastened between both these holes when lifting the engine with the transmission attached. This rigging slants and balances the assembly in a way that allows front-to-back tilting as you lower the transmission through the engine compartment and down under the vehicle.*

5 *It is tempting to use both the lift point mounting holes to install the engine by itself, but doing this raises the rear of the engine assembly and makes engine-to-transmission alignment and connection more difficult. Only use the front 3/8-16 UNC tapped hole when lifting the engine only.*

Engine Drop-in and Connections

Installing the engine in the vehicle takes more care than pulling the engine out. You have to carefully align and insert the front of the transmission into the rear of the crankshaft or into the clutch assembly as you reinstall it. Jacking up the front of the transmission as high as possible and using the correct lifting point(s) on the engine is needed to align the transmission parts to the large engine to bellhousing locating dowel pins.

Proper installation alignment between the engine and transmission is especially important when inserting a manual transmission's input shaft through the clutch disc and into the pilot bushing. Cocking or "side-load" on the transmission's input shaft can bend the clutch disc's center hub as it goes through the splines. A bent clutch disc hub will cause clutch "chatter" in operation.

Focus on getting the engine level and straight as you move the dowel pins into their matching holes. Start a few of the engine to transmission bellhousing bolts once contact is made. Install additional bolts to hold the assemblies together and then set the engine onto the engine mounts. Remove the hoist, then jack up and support the vehicle so the torque converter can be bolted to the flex plate for an automatic transmission.

Install the bellhousing dust cover(s) and secure any other under chassis bolts prior to placing the vehicle on the ground. Move up into the engine compartment and install and assemble all of the other items that were removed during engine removal.

The reassembly order is not that important, with the only exceptions being the radiator and distributor, which we leave until last. For access reasons, install the alternator, power steering pump, pulleys, hoses, and fan and belts before installing the radiator. The distributor will need to be carefully "clocked" to top dead center (TDC) compression stroke, so do the distributor installation as a last step, right before start-up.

Installing the Engine

1 *A portable engine hoist allows engine installation without removing the hood if you keep your lift chain or strap short. Always use a hoist on a hard surface and have the vehicle on its wheels to prevent the possibility of it falling off a jack or jack stands.*

2 *The engine just cleared the radiator yoke and hood with a short strap fastened to the front lift hole. The 30-degree tilt and the front-to-back balance were perfect.*

3 *All of the accessories that were installed on the engine stand cleared, including the TorqStorm supercharger mounting bracket and lower pulley. Watch closely as you lower the engine into position to be sure that it does not catch any wires or hoses, the throttle cable, or the transmission cooler lines.*

4 *Use the two large dowel pins pressed into the back of the engine block as a guide to mate the engine to the bellhousing. The parts will slide together if everything is aligned correctly, but you may want to use a couple of longer bolts or short pieces of all-thread to help guide the pins into the holes. Stop, inspect, and reposition the engine and transmission assembly if they do not go together easily. Never attempt to draw the assemblies together using the bellhousing bolts.*

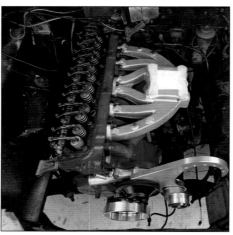

5 *Remove the jack that is supporting the transmission once the bellhousing bolts are installed. Then lower the assembly onto the engine mounts. This engine settled into position without any problems, so we attached the remaining parts and made connections.*

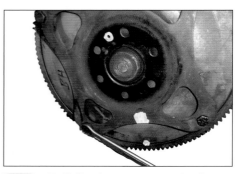

6 *Bolt the torque converter to the flex plate using special thin head bolts. The bolt holes only align one way, with the small 1/8-inch reference hole opposite to the converter drain plug, so mark that position on the front face of the plate. The factory bolts need to be tightened to 25 ft-lbs. These bolts are known to loosen, back out, hit on the rear of the block, and make noise similar to a bearing knock, so threadlock compound is recommended.*

7 *Install and connect the starter motor, alternator, pulleys, cooling system hoses, fan, and fan belt(s) before installing the radiator. This sequence gives you room to work and reduces the chance of damaging the radiator while working inside the engine compartment.*

8 Attach the exhaust head pipe(s) to the manifold(s) and install the carburetor. We made our own custom throttle cable and return spring bracket for the new Aussiespeed intake manifold being tested, but aftermarket versions of a bracket that bolts to the carburetor mounting bolts is available through Summit or JEGS.

9 Attach the throttle cable, fuel supply, hoses, choke, and kickdown (throttle pressure) linkage to the carburetor. TorqueFlite automatic transmissions need throttle pressure, so be sure to connect it. The aftermarket has universal cable actuated throttle pressure kits if you cannot get the mechanical linkage to fit. Do not operate the vehicle without throttle pressure.

10 Install the radiator and connect the transmission cooler lines. The large TorqStorm crankshaft pulley blocked our approach to one of the transmission fluid cooler hard lines, so we had to reroute it to one side.

11 We had to replace the straight flair fitting at the radiator transmission cooler with a 45-degree version and do some minor metal tube bending in order to clear the supercharger's drive pulley. We may decide to install and reroute the transmission fluid cooling to an aftermarket cooler because fan belt access through this area is still tight.

Distributor Installation

The Slant Six distributor is driven by a small gear that engages directly with the camshaft. This gear has 13 teeth, so it is challenging to find the correct installation position that will allow the engine to start. As the old saying goes "Internal combustion engines need three things to run: fuel, compression, and spark . . ." Incorrect distributor installation (incorrect ignition timing) is the most common reason for a "no start" condition when the distributor has been removed and reinstalled on a Slant Six, so pay close attention to the following installation steps.

Installing the Distributor

1 The last item installed is the distributor. Many Slant Six distributors are held in place by a slotted plate and two 7/16 retaining bolts. Be sure to loosen the bottom bolt that holds the slotted plate to the distributor so you can get the maximum ignition timing adjustment travel from the distributor. Late-model engines have a ring and clamp hold-down system that allows more travel range, so use one of those if you can.

2 Set the engine at TDC compression stroke by looking at the timing marks and the valve movements. Watch the front two valve springs while turning the engine over with the starter and align the TDC marks after the intake valve (the second one from the front) has opened and closed. There should be lash clearance at these valves if you are on TDC compression stroke.

3 Apply some moly grease to the distributor gear before installing the unit into the engine. The plastic distributor gear does not need this special grease, but this is a nice way to get more lubricant onto the delicate oil pump drive gear to camshaft gear contact area. Note that the distributor has two O-ring seals: one thin O-ring on the shaft and a larger O-ring at the base of the hold-down plate.

4 The factory installed the Slant Six distributor with the number-1 spark plug terminal in the four o'clock position. This position allows

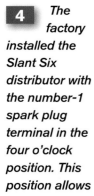

for the most direct spark plug wire routings. The distributor rotates clockwise and the firing order is 1-5-3-6-2-4 for all Slant Six engines. The number-1 spark plug wire terminal is next to the cap's locating notch and hold-down depression, molded into the cap.

5 The static timing method is the best way to set the ignition timing. Place the engine at the desired initial timing position (approximately 10 degrees BTDC). Install an extra spark plug into the number-1 plug wire and ground it to the cylinder head. Energize the ignition system (turn the key to the "Run" position), and then rotate the distributor "back and forth." You should see a spark jump the plug as you cross the correct distributor "trigger" position. Bolt down the distributor at this place and try to start the engine. Reposition the distributor or do additional testing if you do not get a spark across the plug when doing this check.

Fluids and Prestart Checks

Water and engine oil will need to be installed prior to engine start-up. Note that we said water and not coolant because you will want to do your first cooling system fill and engine start-up with plain water to check for leaks and "sweep out" the cooling system. Do this before adding expensive antifreeze or other cooling system additives.

The power steering and transmission fluid should also be checked prior to starting the new engine for the first time. Engine oil needs to be added as well. Pour new oil over all of the valve gear to get those parts well lubricated prior to start-up.

Other prestart checks include checking all wire connections and linkages to be sure everything is installed, tight, and in good working order. The throttle linkage, throttle return spring, and kickdown linkage (if equipped) are especially important and should be checked for full open, full close, and smooth operation before any engine start-up is attempted.

Start-Up and Run-In

The last steps before start-up are installing the engine oil filter, adding oil, and doing final preparations so you can quickly perform tuning adjustments once the engine is running. This is the "magic moment," so do not be in a hurry to start the engine and drive the vehicle. It is better to triple-check everything before attempting to start a new or rebuilt engine.

Our race car already has a set of mechanical gauges, but we like to install oil pressure and temperature gauges underhood so those fluid conditions can be monitored while we set the timing and lash the valves. Our intake manifold had open ports, so we also installed a vacuum gauge. The thermostat cover is a convenient place to install the large fitting needed for a mechanical temperature gauge.

Add water to the cooling system. We use bottled distilled water, but tap water is also okay for the first fill. The goal here is to install an inexpensive fluid into the system so you can check for leaks and also "sweep" any remaining contamination out of the water jackets and radiator prior to adding coolant.

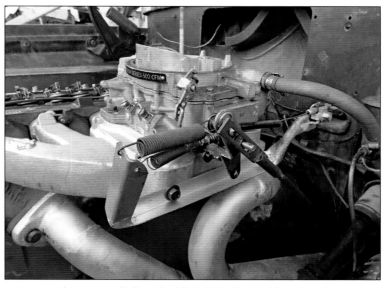

Smooth throttle operation and full return is an absolute must on any vehicle, so triple-check to be sure you can get full throttle open, full close, and smooth motion from the throttle and kickdown linkage. We use two throttle return springs as a fail-safe. You do not want to experience an engine stuck at wide open throttle (WOT) . . . trust me on that.

Precheck, Initial Start-Up, and Post-Start-Up

1 Getting the oil filter to fill up quickly is a big part of getting oil pressure, so put some oil directly into the filter before screwing it onto the engine. Pour about 1/3 of a quart directly into the filter's center hole and then roll the filter around to "wet" all the material inside. Place a pan under the oil filter's mounting location and pour some additional oil into the oil pump itself to help prime the pump.

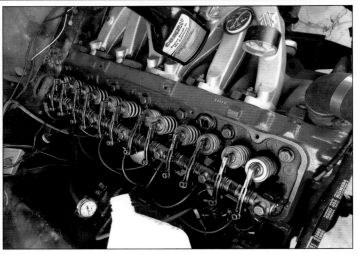

2 Most Slant Six engines take 5 quarts of oil when the oil filter is dry. Add 4 quarts of oil right before engine start-up by pouring the oil over the rocker arms and valve springs. The pressurized oil will take a couple of minutes to make its way up to the valve gear, so wetting those parts now gives them the lubrication they need during initial start-up. Special protective camshaft lobe/ solid lifter additive is installed after the oil by pouring it down each pushrod. We keep 1 quart of oil aside and use it to calibrate the dipstick after the engine starts and the oil filter is full.

3 Use a small squirt bottle of gas to fill the carburetor float bowls. Pouring fuel into the carburetor bowls will allow the engine to start quickly and run instead of having to crank the engine over long enough to pull fuel up from the tank.

4 Ready to attempt start-up? Take one more close look at everything and then squirt some fuel directly into the carburetor and fire up the engine. You may have to adjust the timing and idle speed and repeat this process until the engine starts and stays running. Check to be sure that the engine gets oil pressure within the first 30 seconds of running. If not, shut down the engine, pull the oil filter, and refill it with more oil.

5 It runs! Look under the vehicle once the engine is running and has oil pressure to see if there are any major leaks. There will be some smoke in the engine compartment, mostly from oil and/or paint burning off the exhaust manifold(s) and pipes as it comes up to temperature. Run a fan or let that smoke clear before doing further checks and valve adjustment work.

6 Run the engine between 1,000 and 2,000 rpm for a few minutes to help the cam break in and to warm it up. A faster choke idle speed may be in effect, so disconnect choke linkage or back out the choke's fast idle screw to avoid excessive RPM during initial start-up. Idle down the engine and adjust the timing as needed. Review the oil pressure and temperature to be sure those are normal.

7 Check to see if the rocker arms are all oiling and if every pushrod is spinning. Oil should be running down all the pushrods at this point, so we often touch the top of each rod to wipe away the oil and see the paint mark we put on them.

Precheck, Initial Start-Up, and Post-Start-Up *CONTINUED*

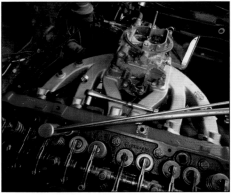

8 *One of the pushrods in our engine was hardly spinning, so we shut the engine off, removed that pushrod, and swapped a different lifter into that position. There are a few different tools that can be used to do this job, but a magnet on a telescopic shaft got the lifter out quickly. Lubricate and reinstall a replacement lifter with a long needle-nose pliers or a hemostat. The replacement lifter spun much better upon restarting the engine.*

9 *Many head gasket manufacturers claim that their gaskets do not require retorquing, but we always check head bolt tightness after the first heat cycle of an engine. We often find that the head bolts do take a little more torque. Also check the intake and exhaust manifold retaining nuts to see if any of those need additional tightening.*

10 *Check and adjust the valve clearances as needed. Factory lash specifications are 0.010 for the intake valves and 0.020 on the exhaust valves. Refer to the previous Mechanical Valve Adjustment section for additional valve adjustment details.*

11 *The last step is to install the valve cover and air cleaner assembly. Use some thread or fine wire through the bolt holes to hold the cover gasket in place as you position the cover and gasket assembly onto the cylinder head.*

Engine Start-Up Checklist

There are a lot of things to keep track of when starting a new engine for the first time. Here is a list of items to watch and check as the engine starts, runs, and does its first heat cycles.

- ❑ Does the engine develop acceptable oil pressure (45 to 55 psi)?
- ❑ Does the temperature stay in the operating range (160 to 200 degrees)?
- ❑ Are there any fluid or vacuum leaks (oil, water, fuel, ATF, etc.)?
- ❑ Are fluid levels correct?
- ❑ Are there any funny noises or excess smoke out the tailpipe?
- ❑ Does the throttle operate smoothly (low idle speed and full open)?
- ❑ Are the head bolts torqued to specification after a heat cycle?
- ❑ Are the valve clearances correct (0.010 intake and 0.020 exhaust or to cam card specs)?
- ❑ Is it at the correct initial timing setting?
- ❑ Have you made sure that the total ignition timing does not exceed 30 degrees?
- ❑ Is the kickdown linkage connected and working smoothly with throttle operation?
- ❑ Will the transmission shift into forward and reverse gear?
- ❑ Have you checked that the engine air filter is clean, the air cleaner assembly is installed, and it clears all linkage parts and the hood?

At this point the engine should be running smoothly, have no leaks, and rev up and idle down when throttle is applied. You are now ready to test-drive the vehicle. ■

Break-In Cycles and Tuning

The first test-drive with a new engine is exciting, but take a moment to safety check the entire vehicle before hitting the road. Our race car had been sitting idle for a year, so it needed a lot more than window washing before we could safely drive it.

Check for a firm brake pedal and correct tire pressure at a minimum, and spend time on any other issues so your first drive is a pleasant experience. Plan a short route on roads that allow you to safely pull off and stop when doing your first drive. There are many different recommendations on how you should break in a new engine, but the most important thing is to make sure the engine holds good oil pressure and does not overheat. The piston rings need to "seat" (wear in), and most of this happens during the first 100 miles (in the first 10 miles with our quarter-mile racer!).

Ring manufacturers recommend that the engine be accelerated at three-quarter throttle to 50 mph and then allowed to coast (decelerate) back down to 20 mph to help suck oil up into the ring packs. Repeat this process three to five times and then drive the vehicle normally in "around town" driving conditions (vary engine speeds in the 2,000 to 3,000 rpm range). Avoid sustained full-throttle operation or constant RPM for the first 500 miles of driving. Avoiding high loads for the first 500 miles is more about giving the bearings and pistons time to wear in and reduce friction that can lead to overheating and/or metal transfer (galling and scuffing). Perform your first oil change before running the new engine at full load for long periods.

All systems are go with good idle vacuum, water temperature at 185 degrees, 55 psi of oil pressure, and a lot of fuel pressure. Time to go for a test-drive!

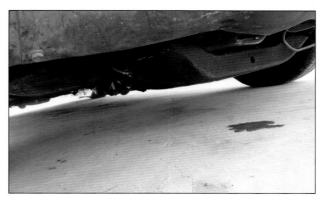

Run the vehicle on a clean surface for a few minutes, then shut the engine off and check for leaks. We had a minor water leak from a radiator hose that we did not tighten well. The good news; no drops of oil or transmission fluid showed up under the car.

The 1962 Lancer is back on the road, but the test drive indicated that it needed additional tuning. Fuel pressure setting, distributor re-curving, and possible carburetor re-jetting was needed to get the most out of the new forced induction setup. These adjustments were made using 91 octane pump gas so the vehicle can be driven on the street as well as at the racetrack.

TorqStorm Supercharger Installation

Our initial road test-drive and engine break-in cycles went fine. We have a smooth, strong-running engine that has 55 psi of oil pressure, 18 inches of vacuum at idle, and no fluid leaks. Based on that, we went right into installing the TorqStorm Supercharger kit onto our fresh motor.

We reviewed all of TorqStorm's installation instructions that were provided in the kit, and we found that we already had some of the needed fuel system upgrade parts on the Lancer, including a 4-barrel intake manifold, carburetor, and high-pressure electric fuel pump. We did have to order a carburetor accelerator pump "marine" seal and a boost-referenced fuel pressure regulator because the carburetor's float bowl needs to be totally sealed, and our current fuel pressure regulator did not have boost pressure reference capability.

Trial Fitting

The kit's mounting brackets and bottom crankshaft pulley were already on the engine, so we mounted the blower unit (compressor) to check clearances and the compressor's outlet position. The supercharger's outlet location is adjustable, so we loosened the scroll's V-band clamp and took the time to check different outlet positions in relation to some other Slant Six intake manifolds.

The latest 4-barrel intake manifolds from Aussiespeed were the first ones we looked at because the short runner version was already on our engine. The older factory Hyper-Pak intake and a couple of other "classic" short-runner Slant Six aftermar-

ket 4-barrel intake manifolds were reviewed next, followed by some multiple carburetor manifolds. The kit's carburetor hat, the large silicone compressor-to-hat connecting hose, and the blow-off valve were also trial fitted during this process to make sure everything would fit together and clear surrounding parts.

The short-runner Aussiespeed intake manifold is 2 inches "outboard" from the factory Slant Six carburetor mounting location, so we had to trim the connection hose to avoid kinking. We loosened the supercharger's scroll and V-band clamp so we could try some other outlet positions.

The legendary Hyper-Pak long-runner "ram-tuned" intake manifold was the first alternate manifold we fit checked. Happy to report that everything should clear and connect once the blower scroll is rotated toward the driver-side inner fender. We will likely check this combination in the near future.

Aussiespeed offers the Hurricane manifold as its long-runner Slant Six intake manifold. Its runners are not as long as the Hyper-Pak, so the scroll outlet moves inward in order to make the connection with the carburetor hat.

There are some "trade-offs" between outlet height and distance to the carburetor hat with the Hurricane. It may require using a slightly longer connecting hose. You can see the length difference between the short and long runners with the Aussiespeed manifolds stacked together.

The short-runner Offenhauser 4-barrel intake and the similar Clifford manifold have carburetor placement near the factory's location, so fitment is good with these units. It is obvious that TorqStorm used this location as the basis for the kit's design.

Supercharger Kit Install Tips

Fuel system improvements and blow-through carburetor sealing was done as part of our installation. In review, the fuel system and carburetor upgrades were the most complicated aspect of the job and the most time consuming. Based on that, you may want to tackle the installation of a 4-barrel induction system and/or installation of a high-pressure fuel pump, fuel lines, and boost-referenced fuel pressure regulator as separate activities before doing the actual supercharger install.

The kit's carburetor hat was designed to be used on a Holley carburetor, so it needed some minor grinding and trimming to fit our old Carter AFB carburetor and clear everything in our Lancer's engine compartment space. We did not check the fit of the supplied hat on a Holley type carburetor, but it should work without the air horn interference we saw with the Carter carburetor (and the newer Edelbrock versions of this carburetor). The carburetor hat did need a fuel regulator pressure reference port drilled and tapped into it, so be prepared to do that work. All said, the kit itself is easy to install, and the performance increase was instantly noticeable.

Installing the Supercharger

1 There are seven 3/8–16 UNC socket head cap screws and washers that hold the compressor unit to the mounting brackets. Be sure to start all these fasteners before tightening and torquing them to 30 ft-lbs. In hindsight, we should have installed the compressor when the radiator was out for better access to the bolts.

2 We installed the drive belt once the compressor was in place. Position the belt, swing the spring-loaded tensioner pulley toward the passenger fender with a wrench, and then slip the belt into its groove. The bigger 4-inch pulley needed a longer belt, which we got from TorqStorm.

3 The blowoff valve mounts directly onto a "bib" that is welded onto the compressor's scroll. Be sure to lubricate the O-ring inside the 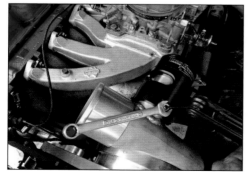 blowoff valve's bore so it slides on easily and fully seats. Tighten the three hold-down set screws and locknuts to ensure that the unit stays firmly in place under boost.

4 We made a section of 1/4-inch hard metal line to run from the manifold port to the blowoff valve, then we used a short piece of pressure-rated  rubber hose and clamps to make the final connection at the valve's nipple. The goal here was to have a heat-resistant and problem-free signal connection to the blowoff valve.

Installing the Supercharger *CONTINUED*

5 Most blow-through supercharger carburetors are based on the Holley design, but our race car has a bare-bones Carter AFB that has no vacuum fittings or choke. We decided to use this carburetor for testing after adding a special seal to the accelerator pump shaft to keep pressure from leaking out of the float bowl area.

6 Edelbrock offers a marine accelerator pump seal kit that comes with a modern pump plunger, a pump stem seal, and a retaining clip. Lucky for us, these parts also fit the older Carter AFB carburetor that we were using.

7 Pull out the step-up rod and piston assemblies and disconnect the accelerator pump linkage before removing the top of the carburetor. Install the pump seal so the raised lip faces the float bowl area and push on the retaining clip. We applied a little silicone grease to the pump's shaft and seal lip to keep everything sliding smoothly as we reassembled the carb.

8 Our carburetor had some slight interference between the air horn and the supercharger's hat, especially around the step-up rod towers. We marked these locations and took some measurements to see how much grinding would be needed to make the needed clearance.

9 A small amount of material was removed from three places around the edge of the hat to allow it to fit onto the carburetor's air horn. We also drilled holes and tapped one with 1/16 and the other with 1/8 NPT pipe threads to accept a hose bib or other fittings.

10 *A one-to-one boost-referenced fuel regulator is recommended when using forced induction, so we added one to our fuel system. TorqStorm instructions say to take the reference signal out of the carburetor hat, so we had to modify the hat to do that.*

11 *We change to a vacuum and pressure (boost) gauge inside the vehicle, so a plastic tube had to be connected to the intake manifold. We had some extra manifold ports to use, but we did have to use a reducer fitting to make the connection.*

12 *The 90-degree silicone hose used between the supercharger's outlet and the carburetor hat was longer than we needed for the short-runner Aussiespeed intake manifold we were using.*

13 *The 90-degree hose had to be trimmed on both ends to make it fit well, so we marked it and used a sharp pair of scissors to do the cutting. The silicone hoses supplied in this kit are stiff and tough; use care when cutting. We used a little silicone grease to help push the hose ends onto their respective parts.*

14 *We used a 1/8 thread hose fitting in the side of the hat to connect the boost referenced fuel pressure regulator to a pressure source. An extra-long piece of hose was used to make sure there was enough hose to flex as the engine torqued around during hard acceleration.*

Installing the Supercharger CONTINUED

15 We changed supercharger drive pulleys a few times during our testing, and this required removing the compressor unit from the Lancer's small engine compartment. The drive pulley is pressed onto the shaft and has two keys, so using a strong jaw-type puller is a must.

16 The kit provides a K&N air filter, aluminum tubing, hose, and clamps needed to install an air cleaner assembly onto the supercharger's intake port.

17 The installed air cleaner and tubing was a tight fit with the air filter itself ending up right over the steering box. The exhaust system is close by, so our short-term plan was to install a heat shield to protect the air filter from excessive exhaust pipe heat. Running additional ducting to deliver cooler outside air is something we want to do as a later upgrade to the system.

18 The Lancer race car runs well with a basically stock Slant Six, an Aussiespeed intake manifold, Dutra Dual exhaust manifolds, and the TorqStorm supercharger running 6 psi of boost. The best time so far has been 13.50, but we still need more tuning and track time to dial in the setup.

Supercharger Testing

TorqStorm offers different compressor pulley sizes to adjust the amount of boost the system develops, so we requested all sizes for testing. The 4-inch pulley (the least amount of boost at 5 psi) was the first one tested, and then we progressed to the 3.5 and 3.25 sizes.

The first test-drive with the supercharger was done on our local highway. We quickly discovered that the increased power level combined with our "interesting-looking" (and loud) vehicle was asking for trouble. We decided to do additional testing at the local drag strip, where we could collect better data in a safe environment. It is interesting how a scary-fast street car does not seem as fast once you have it at the racetrack, but that is exactly what we experienced once the Lancer was at the drag strip.

Our first pass down the drag strip started off fine, but the engine pinged at high RPM, then surged and misfired at the end of the pass due to low fuel pressure (our fuel gauge went down to 2 psi). We backed the timing down to 26 degrees total, adjusted the idle back up to 800 rpm, and increased the idle fuel pressure setting from 8 to 10 psi for the next run. The next pass produced a 13.98 quarter-mile time at 94.56 mph with the boost pressure reading 4 psi on our in-car pressure gauge. The fuel pressure was dropping as we went through the "traps," so we increased the regulator pressure to 12 psi for the next pass. The next run down the track produced a 13.94 at 95.39 mph.

We changed over to the 3.5-inch compressor pulley at this point. The next run showed a two-tenths improvement of 13.75 at 96.63 mph. Our 60-foot times were in the 2.0 to higher 1.9 range, so the car could use some help in getting off the starting line faster. The next pass was slower, at 14.08, so we did some checking and found that the O-ring between the carburetor and the hat was bulged out and leaking boost pressure. That slow pass eliminated the car from the track's bracket race program, so we went home to fix the pressure leak and prepare for a return trip to the drag strip.

Back at the shop, we reviewed the O-ring to hat seal and looked at different ways to get a more-robust seal around the 5-inch diameter Carter carburetor air horn. The 0.087 cross-section O-ring supplied with the kit seemed small for our needs, so we decided to make a larger flat gasket out of 3/32 thick silicone material we had. Some measuring and a sharp pair of scissors produced our replacement hat gasket. The flat gasket was much easier to deal with once it was trimmed and fitted to the carburetor. We glued it down to the carburetor just to be sure it did not shift around or get misplaced while the hat was off. In hindsight, a high-quality 5-inch air cleaner base gasket would have likely solved the problem with a lot less work.

The plan for the next drag strip outing was to make a pass with the repaired carburetor hat seal and the 3.5-inch drive pulley and then

We made a hat gasket out of 0.093-inch thick silicone rubber material by tracing it and carefully cutting it out with scissors. A standard 5-inch air cleaner gasket can also be used, but be sure it fits well and is clamped down firmly to prevent boost pressure leaks.

The 5-inch-diameter carburetor to carburetor hat sealing O-ring bulged out and created a pressure leak as boost levels were increased. Using a Carter AFB carburetor instead of a Holley is the likely reason behind this issue. We changed to a flat gasket to solve the problem.

We glued the new hat gasket in place with weatherstrip adhesive to reduce the chance of the gasket slipping out of place under boost pressure. We found that the carburetor to hat sealing point was the most problematic in our system, so we fit checked and carefully assembled the hat to carburetor seal to keep it from leaking or blowing out.

change to the 3.25-inch pulley size to see if that change would generate additional boost and improve the elapsed times.

The first run was impressive with a 13.70 at 96.82 mph. That pass told us that the new hat seal gasket was doing its job. We went ahead and changed to the 3.25 pulley. Doing this pulley change required compressor removal, a gear puller, and a shorter belt with the smaller pulley. In hindsight, we should have waited and made a few more runs before changing pulleys because we missed the next "time trial" pass by making this change so early in the event.

The first run on the smallest pulley got us a 13.55 at 97.59 mph . . . nice! The boost pressure reading on our gauge was now higher, pushing its way up to 6 psi in the higher RPM. The next run was just like the previous pass but with a slightly better time of 13.50 at 97.77 mph.

The bad news was that this pass was the first round of the bracket race, and we red lit by 0.020 of a second, which eliminated the car for the night. We packed up and headed home, thinking about the next step(s) needed to make the car go faster. One thing was certain: we got a lot of compliments on our blown "road toad" and its overall performance!

The supercharger setup has a lot of wow factor when you open the car's hood, so now we want to swap the intake manifold to the long ram Hyper-Pak to really get people talking! Another thought was to add a little nitrous shot to help the car leave the starting line quicker and "harder." We wonder if the nitrous will act as a chemical intercooler and help cool the intake charge for some additional power. Looks like more drag strip testing is in our future!

The 1962 Lancer waits in the staging lanes for another run down the drag strip. A friend came out with his early Valiant so we had two road toads making passes down the strip.

The supercharged Lancer gets ready to make another run. We are impressed that the TorqStorm blower makes good power and produces consistent time slips, which is important when doing bracket racing.

Supercharger Pulley Size Versus ET

Pulley Size	Quarter-Mile Time	MPH
4.0 inches	13.98	94.56
4.0 inches	13.94	95.39
3.5 inches	13.75	96.63
3.5 inches	14.08	Let-off
3.5 inches	13.70	96.82
3.25 inches	13.55	97.59
3.25 inches	13.50	97.77

Summary

The TorqStorm Supercharger kit does well on a stock compression (8.5:1) Slant Six, and it is a relatively easy kit to install. The biggest issue is the need for an upgraded fuel system and a special sealed carburetor. The other consideration is the fact that this type of supercharger is limited in the amount of boost that it will produce. The power gain the system provides is impressive, and it will not hurt a factory Slant Six, as long as the system is installed correctly. Adequate fuel pressure and 24 to 26 degrees total ignition timing under boost conditions are essential.

My personal thank you to all the Slant Six enthusiasts who help keep this durable and interesting engine in service. Congratulations to everyone who has taken on the big job of rebuilding an engine and the work needed to keep an older vehicle on the road. Not many people in our current instant-gratification, throw-away culture will want to do a long, complex rebuilding or automotive restoration project, so know that you are one of a select few who can claim internal combustion engine rebuilding as part of their "life experience."

The work covered here does not stop once the engine is running and the vehicle is on the road. We all know there will be ongoing maintenance, such as oil changes and tune-ups. More important, you should always be thinking about fine-tuning your engine to extract the most power and efficiency. Experimenting with valve clearance settings, recurving the distributor, and fine-tuning the carburetor jetting are good examples. This type of work will likely lead to other bolt-on accessories or replacing items with higher-quality parts as projects of their own.

The reality is that your engine rebuild, start-up, and break-in efforts are only the start of the journey. The trip will continue, so embrace and enjoy the process as you go. Try to connect with other like-minded Slant Six owners by visiting forums such as the ones at slantsix.org and inlinersinternational.org. Joining a local car club and attending car shows or racing events are other great ways to enjoy the automotive hobby and connect with fellow automotive enthusiasts. Again, thank you for your support and interest in the Chrysler Slant Six, and I hope to see you on the on the slantsix.org message board or at a Slant Six event.

ENGINE REBUILD CHECKLIST EXAMPLE

Here is a sample checklist you can use as a starting point for your list:

Machine Shop
- ❏ Engine block (cleaned and machined)
- ❏ Camshaft bearings (installed)
- ❏ Crankshaft and bearings (correct size and type)
- ❏ Piston and connecting rods (cleaned, machined, and assembled)
- ❏ Cylinder head (cleaned, machined, and assembled)
- ❏ Sheet metal, fasteners, and oil pickup tube (cleaned)
- ❏ Manifolds (resurfaced or replaced)
- ❏ Radiator (serviced or replaced)

Purchased Parts
- ❏ Piston rings
- ❏ Camshaft and lifters

- ❏ Timing set and oil slinger
- ❏ Oil, water, and fuel pumps (if needed)
- ❏ Freeze plugs
- ❏ Gasket set and sealers (RTV, pipe dope, and adhesive)
- ❏ Spark plugs and wires (if needed)
- ❏ Thermostat (if needed)

Supplies
- ❏ Grease and lubricants (assembly lube, moly grease, anti-seize and spray lube)
- ❏ Plastigauge: in sizes green (0.001 to 0.003) and red (0.002 to 0.006)
- ❏ Spray paint
- ❏ Hoses and belts (if needed)
- ❏ Oil, air, and fuel filters
- ❏ Antifreeze and coolant
- ❏ Engine oil
- ❏ Cam break-in additive (optional) ∎

Bolt Size and Tightening Information for 170, 198, and 225 Slant Six Engines					
Fastener Location	Thread Size	Torque (ft-lbs)	Wrench Size	Underhead length (inches)	Notes
Connecting rod bolt/nut*	3/8-24	45	9/16	9/16 thick nut	
Cylinder head bolt*	7/16-14	70	11/16	4.3	Cast iron
Main bearing cap*	1/2-13	85	3/4	3.0	Cast iron
Camshaft to timing gear*	7/16-14	35	5/8	1.4	ARP 155-1002
Timing chain cover bolts**	5/16-18	200 in-lbs	1/2	0.6 (automatic transmission pan bolt)	
Engine to transmission bellhousing (4)	3/6-16	30	9/16	1.5 (frontside bolt is 1.75)	
Engine to transmission bellhousing, bottom(2)	7/16-14	35	5/8	2.0	
Transmission brace to transmission bellhousing**	3/8-16	25	9/16	1.0	
Transmission brace to engine block	7/16-14	35	5/8	1.0	
Rear main seal retainer**	3/6-16	30	3/8	3.0	12 pt., small 9/16-inch diameter head
Valve cover bolts**	1/4-20	40 in-lbs	7/16	0.5	
Distributor clamp**	1/4-20	95 in-lbs	7/16	0.5	
Engine mount to frame nut	1/2-13	85	3/4	0.6	With captive washer
Engine mount bracket to block	7/16-14	45	5/8	1.5	
Flywheel to crankshaft	7/16-20	55	5/8	0.875	5/8-inch-thick head
Flex plate to crankshaft*	7/16-20	55	3/4	0.5	ARP 200-2903
Flex plate to converter*	5/16-24	270 in-lbs	9/16 (short)	0.450	ARP 240-7301
Fan attaching bolts**	5/16-18	200 in-lbs	1/2	Length based on spacer	
Fuel pump attaching bolts**	3/8-16	20	9/16	1.5	
Bellhousing bottom cover**	5/16-18	7	1/2	0.6 (automatic transmission pan bolt)	
Alternator bracket to block (2)**	3/8-16	30	9/16	1.25	1 bolt 5/16-18 x 1.5
Alternator adjustor strap to head**	3/8-16	20	9/16	0.5	
Intake to exhaust manifold (3)**	5/16-18	240 in-lbs	1/2	3.0 minimum	
Manifold set to head studs**	5/16-18 x 1/2, 5/16-24 x 3/4, 1¾ total, use sealer into head				
Oil pan drain plug**	1/2-20	20	7/8	0.5	
Oil pan bolts (6 longer at ends)**	5/16-18	200 in-lbs	1/2	0.6 (automatic transmission pan bolts)	
Oil pump mounting bolts**	5/16-18	200 in-lbs	1/2	1.625	
Starter mounting bolts	7/16-14	40	5/8	1.5	Locating stud used
Water pump to block**	3/8-16	25	9/16	1.5	2 bolts at 2.50 inches long
Thermostat cover**	3/8-16	20	9/16	1.0	
Vibration dampener bolt (press)	3/4-16	135	1.25	2.3	1.5 minimum thread

*Indicates fasteners that have an ARP part number for a premium-quality replacement fastener.
**Indicates reference torque only. "Common sense" hand tool tighten, no torque wrench required.

SLANT SIX DISTRIBUTOR

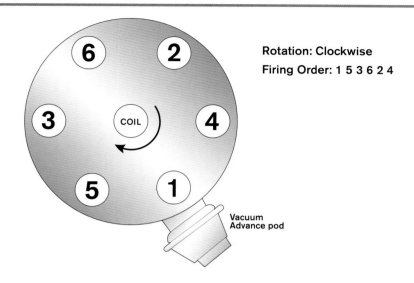

Rotation: Clockwise

Firing Order: 1 5 3 6 2 4

Vacuum
Advance pod

SLANT SIX HEAD TORQUE PATTERN

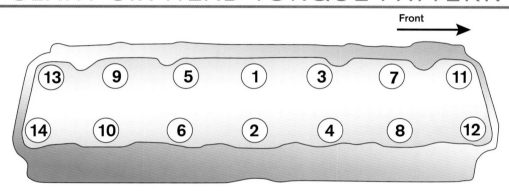

Front

SLANT SIX INTAKE/EXHAUST MANIFOLD TORQUE SEQUENCE

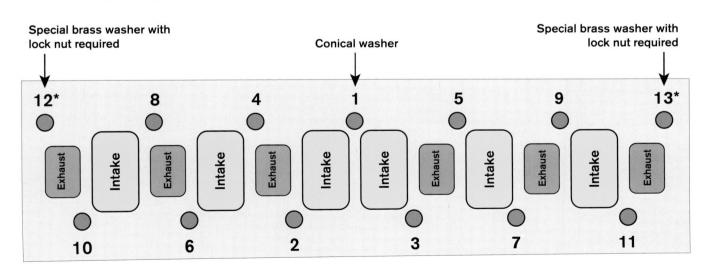

Special brass washer with lock nut required

Conical washer

Special brass washer with lock nut required

— 15 ft-lbs max

— Edges of washers should NOT contact manifolds

Accel
10601 Memphis Ave., #12
Cleveland, OH 44144
216-658-6413
holley.com/brands/accel

ARP
1863 Eastman Ave.
Ventura, CA 93003
800-826-3045
arp-bolts.com

Aussiespeed (Australia)
www.aussiespeedshop.com
Small Town Speed (US Dealer)
972-989-4003

Automotive Electric Services
202 Cty. Rd. 480
Negaunee, MI 49866
906-475-7772
autoelec.com

Centerforce Clutches
2266 Crosswind Dr.
Prescott, AZ 86301
928-771-8422
centerforce.com

Cloyes Performance Products
7800 Ball Rd.
Ft. Smith, AR 72908
479-646-1662
cloyes.com

Comp Cams
3406 Democrat Rd.
Memphis, TN 38118
800-999-8538
compcams.com

Crower Cams & Equipment
6180 Business Center Ct.
San Diego, CA 92154
619-661-6477
crower.com

D. Elgin Racing Cams
1808-D Emiper Industrial Ct.
Santa Rosa, CA 95403
707-545-6115

Falcon Performance
601-696-2161
internalengineparts.com

Federal-Mogul
26451 Crown Valley Pkwy.,
#220
Mission Viejo, CA 92691
949-367-9180
federalmogul.com

Grant Piston Rings
1360 N. Jefferson St.
Anaheim, CA 92807
714-996-0050
grantpistonrings.com

Hastings Manufacturing
Company
325 N. Hanover St.
Hastings, MI 49058
800-776-1088
hastingspistonrings.com

Isky Racing Cams
16020 S. Broadway
Gardena, CA 90248
310-217-9232
iskycams.com

Jack Clifford's Performance
22850 Sheffield Ct.
Wildomar, CA 92595
951-471-1161
cliffordperformance.net

JE Pistons
8 Mason
Irvine, CA 92618
714-898-9763
jepistons.com

K1 Technologies
7201 Industrial Park Blvd.
Mentor, OH 44060-5396
440-951-6600
800-321-1364
k1technologies.com

Kanter Auto Products
76 Monroe St.
Boonton, NJ 07005
800-526-1096
kanter.com

King Bearings
371 Little Falls Rd., Ste. 5
Cedar Grove, NJ 07009
800-772-3670
kingbearings.com

JEGS High Performance
101 JEGS Place
Delaware, OH 43015
800-345-4545
jegs.com

L.A. Sleeve
12051 Rivera Rd.
Santa Fe Springs, CA 90670
800-822-6005
lasleeve.com

Mahle Motorsports
270 Rutledge Rd., Unit C
Fletcher, NC 28732
888-255-1942
us.mahle.com

Mallory Ignition
10601 Memphis Ave., #12
Cleveland, OH 44144
216-658-6413
holley.com/brands/mallory

Manley Performance Products
1960 Swarthmore Ave.
Lakewood, NJ 08701
800-526-1362
manleyperformance.com

Manley West
634 D North Poplar St.
Orange, CA 92868
714-978-3335

McLeod
1600 Sierra Madre Cir.
Placentia, CA 92870
714-630-2764
mcleodracing.com

Melling Engine Parts
2620 Saradan Dr.
Jackson, MI 49202
517-787-8172
melling.com

Molnar Technologies
616-940-4640
molnartechnologies.com

MSD/Autotronic Controls Corp.
1350 Pullman Dr., Dock #14
El Paso, TX 79936
915-857-5200
msdignition.com

Offenhauser Sales
5300 Alhambra Ave.
Los Angeles, CA 90032
323-225-1307
offenhausersales.com

Quick Time
10601 Memphis Ave., #12
Cleveland, OH 44144
216-658-6413
holley.com/brands/quick_time

Pertronix Performance
  Products
440 East Arrow Hwy.
San Dimas, CA 91773
909-599-5955
pertronix.com

Ross Racing Pistons
625 S. Douglas St.
El Segundo, CA 90245
800-392-7677
rosspistons.com

Selby & Sons Engine Machine
3181 Coffey Ln.
Santa Rosa, CA 95403
707-526-4767

Summit Racing
PO Box 909
Akron, OH 44309
800-230-3030
summitracing.com

TorqStorm Superchargers
Accelerated Racing Products
3001 Madison SE
Wyoming, MI 49548
616-706-5580
torqstorm.com

Wiseco Piston
7201 Industrial Park Blvd.
Mentor, OH 44060
800-321-1364
wiseco.com